High
on a
Wing

9/18/9

Byron,

Because a trip is worth
a thousand pictures, may
you find encouragement
and many opportunities to
hit the highways and also
hike to some highpoints.

Jim Mick

High on a Wing

001563

A Motorcyclist's
Travel Log to,
and Trivia About,
Highpoints

Jim Mick

RIW Publishing
Macomb, Michigan

Published by RIW Publishing
56750 Fairchild Road
Macomb, MI 48042

Publisher's Cataloging-in-Publication Data
Mick, James Owen.
    High on a wing: a motorcyclist's travel log to, and trivia about,
    highpoints / James Owen Mick — Macomb, Mich.: RIW
    Publishing, 2001.
       p. cm.
    ISBN 0-9707214-0-4

    1. Mick, James Owen—Journeys. 2. Motorcyclists—United States—
    Travel. 3. Motorcyclists—United States—Biography.
    4. Motorcycling—United States. 5. United States—Description
    and travel. I. Title.

GV1059 52 .M53 2001   2000-193270
629.284/75/092   B—dc21   CIP

05 04 03 02 01 ⚡ 5 4 3 2 1

Project Coordination by Jenkins Group, Inc. • www.bookpublishing.com

Printed in the United States of America

Contents

High On a Wing Itinerary . . . . *vii*

Itinerary Notes . . . . *x*

Introduction . . . . *xi*

01   Mount Marcy, New York 1

02   Mount Mansfield, Vermont 7

03   Mount Washington, New Hampshire 12

04   Mount Katahdin, Maine 22

05   Jerimoth Hill, Rhode Island 28

06   Mount Greylock, Massachusetts 32

07   Mount Frissell, Connecticut 38

08   High Point, New Jersey 40

09   Ebright Azimuth, Delaware 44

10   Spruce Knob, West Virginia 49

11   Backbone Mountain, Maryland 54

12   Mount Davis, Pennsylvania 59

13   Campbell Hill, Ohio .64

14   Hoosier High Point, Indiana 68

15   Black Mountain, Kentucky 73

16   Mount Rogers, Virginia 75

17   Mount Mitchell, North Carolina 78

18   Clingmans Dome, Tennessee 81

19   Sassafras Mountain, South Carolina 86

20   Brasstown Bald, Georgia 89

CONTENTS

21   Cheaha Mountain, Alabama 93

22   Britton Hill, Florida 95

23   Woodall Mountain, Mississippi 97

24   Taum Sauk Mountain, Missouri 99

25   Magazine Mountain, Arkansas 104

26   Driskill Mountain, Louisiana 110

27   Guadalupe Peak, Texas .113

28   Mount Elbert, Colorado 123

29   Mount Sunflower, Kansas 130

30   Black Mesa, Oklahoma .135

31   Wheeler Peak, New Mexico 140

32   Humphreys Peak, Arizona 144

33   Mount Whitney, California 149

34   Boundary Peak, Nevada 153

35   Mount Hood, Oregon 155

36   Mount Rainier, Washington 157

37   Borah Peak, Idaho 164

38   Granite Peak, Montana .171

39   Gannett Peak, Wyoming 175

40   Kings Peak, Utah 181

41   Panorama Point, Nebraska 184

42   Harney Peak, South Dakota 187

43   White Butte, North Dakota 191

44   High Point, Iowa 194

45   Charles Mound, Illinois 198

46   Timms Hill, Wisconsin .201

47   Eagle Mountain, Minnesota 205

48   Mount Arvon, Michigan 208

49   Epilogue 215

      Waiver agreement for Black Mountain 217

High On A Wing Itinerary 1997

ARRIVAL				State	Highpoint & Elevation	Depart	TO NEXT HP		
Actual	Planned						Hrs	Miles	Actual
Trip will begin from Macomb, MI						7am 7/7	17	670	576
IT	noon	7/8	T	NY	Mt. Marcy 5,344'	3pm 7/8	2	80	102
6pm-	6pm	7/8	T	VT	Mt. Mansfield 4,393'	7am 7/9	3+	140	116
10am+	10am+	7/9	W	NH	Mt. Washington 6,288'	2pm- 7/9	6+	260	228
NP	8pm	7/9	W	ME	Mt. Katahdin 5,267'	7am 7/10	12	470	408
6pm-	8pm	7/10	T	*RI	Jerimoth Hill 812'	7am 7/11	4	150	174
3pm-	11am	7/11	F	MA	Mt. Greylock 3,487'	2pm 7/11	1+	50	62
7pm+	4pm	7/11	F	CT	Mt. Frissell 2,380'	7am+ 7/12	3+	140	147
11am+	11am	7/12	S	*NJ	High Point 1,803'	2pm 7/12	5	190	166
8pm-	7pm	7/12	S	DE	Ebright Azimuth 442'	7am 7/14	8	320	343
1pm-	3pm	7/14	M	*WV	Spruce Knob 4,861'	6pm 7/14	1+	60	66
4pm-	7pm+	7/14	M	MD	Backbone Mtn. 3,360'	8am 7/15	2	90	67
<6pm+	10am	7/15	T	PA	Mt. Davis 3,213'	1pm 7/15	7	280	300
>9am-	8pm	7/15	T	*OH	Campbell Hill 1,549'	7am 7/16	2+	100	100

Actual	Planned			State	Highpoint & Elevation	Depart	Hrs	Miles	Actual
2pm-	9am+	7/16	W	*IN	Hoosier High Point 1257'	Noon 7/16	8	320	358
>11pm-	8pm	7/16	W	KY	Black Mtn. 4139'	6am 7/17	3	110	135
Lx2	10am	7/17	T	VA	Mt. Rogers 5729'	Noon 7/17	3	110	152
9pm-	4pm	7/17	T	NC	Mt. Mitchell 6684'	5pm 7/17	2	90	123
>11pm	8pm	7/17	T	TN	Clingmans Dome 6643'	7am 7/18	2	90	113
3pm+	10am	7/18	F	SC	Sassafras Mtn. 3560'	1pm 7/18	4	130	120
7pm+	5pm	7/18	F	GA	Brasstown Bald 4784'	7am 7/19@	4+	180	197
noon-	10am+	7/19	S	AL	Cheaha Mtn. 2405'	1pm+7/19	5+	220	210
HD	7pm	7/19	S	FL	Britton Hill 345'	6am 7/21	9	360	
2<6pm-	3pm	7/21	M	MS	Woodall Mtn. 806'	6pm 7/21	8	320	322
2<2pm-	9am	7/22	T	MO	Taum Sauk Mtn. 1772'	11am 7/22	9	370	480
<9pm	8pm	7/22	T	*AR	Magazine Mtn. 2753'	7am 7/23	8	310	276
<5pm-	3pm	7/23	W	*LA	Driskill Mtn. 535'	6pm 7/23@	19	780	785
10am-	8pm	7/24	T	TX	Guadalupe Peak 8749'	5am 7/25	16	640	639
>11am-	9pm	7/25	F	*CO	Mt. Elbert 14,433'	7am 7/28	8	310	280
RC	3pm	7/28	M	KS	Mt. Sunflower 4039'	6pm 7/28	5	200	258
10am-	10am	7/29	T	OK	Black Mesa 4973'	1pm 7/29	5	200	210

ARRIVAL — TO NEXT HP

NP	7/29	T	6pm	NM	Wheeler Peak 13,161'	6am	7/30	12	480	507
NP	7/30	W	7pm	AZ	Humphreys Peak 12,633'	3am	7/31@	13	540	540
NP	7/31	T	3pm	CA	Mt. Whitney 14,494'	5am+	8/1	2+	100	127
NP	8/1	F	8am	NV	Boundary Peak 13,140'	11am	8/1	21	820	738
NP	8/2	S	12am	OR	Mt. Hood 11,239'	2pm	8/2	5	220	294
NP	8/2	S	7pm	*WA	Mt. Rainier 14,410'	10am	8/4@	17	660	680
NP	8/5	T	4pm	ID	Borah Peak 12,662'	8am	8/6	8	300	379
NP	8/6	W	4pm	MT	Granite Peak 12,799'	8am	8/7	7	280	386
NP	8/7	T	4pm	WY	Gannett Peak 13,804'	9am	8/8	6	220	250
NP	8/8	F	3pm	UT	Kings Peak 13,528'	6am	8/9	12	470	392
10am+	8/9	S	6pm	NE	Panorama Pt. 5424'	7am	8/11	7	270	547
BW	8/11	M	2pm	SD	Harney Peak 7242'	5pm	8/11	5	210	230
<4pm+	8/12	T	10am	ND	White Butte 3506'	1pm	8/12@	14	540	558
9am+	8/13	W	noon	IA	High Point 1670'	3pm	8/13	9	350	362
<5pm+	8/14	T	10am	IL	Charles Mound 1235'	noon	8/14	6	250	291
11am	8/14	T	6pm	*WI	Timms Hill 1951'	8am	8/15	8	320	305
noon+	8/15	F	4pm	MN	Eagle Mtn. 2301'	8am	8/16@	9	360	365
L	8/16	S	6pm	*MI	Mt. Arvon 1979'	7am	8/17	14	550	637
8pm	8/17	Sunday			HOME at Macomb, MI			**Total Miles:**	14,680	15,333

Itinerary Notes:

*	Special Events (planned before departure)	11
@	Crossing time zone	6
<	Day early	7
>	Day late	4
IT	Insufficient Time to make the climb	1
NP	Not planned to make the climb	11
L	Lost, did not find the summit	2
HD	Hurricane Danny prevented me	1
RC	Road Closed	1
BW	Bad Weather	1

Statistics:

Actually stood on 31 summits

Visited 47 states

320 gallons of gas (avg cost $1.257/gal)

Total cost $402.51

47.9 mpg (22.3 mpg estimated @ 95 mph)

Introduction
It's her fault, she started it!

At the 1995 Honda Hoot in Asheville, North Carolina, my wife and I bought two engraved plastic items. The one for Jeri's jacket explained her "Hairdo By Honda," and the other was a map of the U.S. for our 1994 Honda Gold Wing, Interstate, with the words, "On A Wing and A Prayer" along with our names. That was our first trip outside Michigan on our new Gold Wing, but as I started gluing glass diamonds on the states we had just passed through, Jeri said, "It seems that we should accomplish something in a state before you claim credit for having been there on our Wing."

"Something like visiting the state capitol?" I said with a bit of sarcasm in my question. She dislikes downtown riding as much as I dislike downtown driving.

"No, but just being on a stretch of road through a part of the state is not much of an accomplishment. Did we even stop in Virginia or Tennessee?" she continued.

We had been on US-23, which crosses only about 60 miles of the western tip of Virginia and maybe 70 miles through Tennessee. She had a point, and I recalled the saying, "Appear stupid by saying nothing, rather than opening your mouth and removing all doubt."

Jeri was looking at my road atlas as she continued to make a point. "Your maps identify capitals, largest cities and highest points. In North Carolina, the highest point is Mt. Mitchell, which isn't far from here. Didn't we go there with the boys in the late '70s?"

Her memory has always been better than mine, but even I recalled the photographs we took of our boys wrapped in beach towels, and the butterfly on the trail, and it seems like someone was buried at the summit. I wasn't ignoring her by not answering her last question. I think I was still trying to figure out if we had stopped in either Virginia or Tennessee, so I was just a question behind.

"The highest point would usually be a hill or a mountain, but what about states like Florida?" I still had a bit of sarcasm in my voice.

She flipped the pages of the atlas to Florida. "It says it's just 345 feet and in Walton County." She located the coordinates and said, "Here it is. It's marked with a little triangle, gives the elevation again, and says highest point in Florida."

That's how Jeri started it, and like a blood hound given a scent, I began the quest for going to the highest natural elevation in each of the contiguous states, a goal that occupied most of my available time for the next two years. If you have ever been involved in planning a big event, you understand how plans evolve. Early in the process, I had called state tourism departments to request information about their highpoints. The term, "highpoint," is generally accepted as, and used in this book to refer to the highest natural elevation of a state as officially recognized by the U.S. Geological Survey publication, *Elevations and Distances in the United States.* I was surprised that information was not easy to discover, but as my quest continued, some interesting information started coming in. I discovered the Highpointers Club, which allows membership to any individual interested in climbing or promoting climbing of the highest point in each of the 50 states. Members are called *Highpointers* and receive the *Apex to Zenith (A to Z) Newsletter* quarterly. The mailman was becoming a more-welcomed visitor than normal, and I visited our local library as if working on a college term paper.

The first of nearly 100 newspaper articles I researched for this book had one minor error. I discovered that newspapers are often in error, so whenever possible I have attempted to verify the information I used. That first article was in the *Detroit Free Press* dated October 25, 1993, where Emilia Askari reported that until 1992, maps incorrectly listed Mt. Curwood in Baraga County as Michigan's highest elevation. A few months after making that note, I looked at my parents' old *Road Atlas* from 1988, which showed Mt. Arvon as the highest point. How could that be? Simple, just one digit in the article was wrong. It incorrectly reported 1992 instead of the correct year of 1982!

Finally the basic plan of visiting each of the 48 contiguous state highpoints on one six-week trip was in place. Jeri would stay at home to coordinate plans and be the one point of contact while I was getting high on our Gold Wing.

One day while picking out interesting history and trivia about highpoints and sharing it with Jeri, she said I should write a book about my trip to share the information I uncovered. Jeri not only started it, but has also given me the occasional encouragement to follow through on this monumental but very exciting project. I have a new appreciation for any writer who gets his book published and could not even guess how many hours have been spent to give you what you hold in your hands. ENJOY!

#01

Mount Marcy, New York
(5,344 feet)

Cotton: Good on the bike, poor on the hike.

PLANS FOR THIS TRIP of a lifetime had been in the making for two years. I had planned to leave Monday morning, July 7, 1997 at 7 am, but those plans were changed. On Sunday, the day before, several friends gathered at our home for a farewell picnic followed by a special program at our church that evening. People who live in Michigan often explain where they live by pointing to a place at the back of their left hand since Michigan resembles a mitten. We live near the knuckle at the base of your thumb, which is about 30 miles northeast of Detroit. During the six-mile ride from the picnic to the church, we ran into a summer shower—just enough to get the bikes dirty.

Knowing the Gold Wing would become dirty on the 15,000-mile trip, which lay ahead, was not reason enough to begin the trip with the milky evidence of Sunday's ride in the rain. The weather for my first day promised to be very nice, so I was up by 6:30 am with the thermometer indicating only 50 degrees outside. I washed our Gold Wing and was ready for the road by 10:15 am. The odometer read 37,304, and the temperature had moved up to 60 degrees.

Our youngest son Jason and his friend Brian Boers did not work that Monday, so when they heard that my departure was being delayed, they arrived about 9:30 am to start the trip with me. I don't mind riding alone, but when the ride is good, having the boys' headlights shining in my mirrors, or following their taillights makes it even more enjoyable.

Jeri took a picture of us just before we left the driveway and headed north. We stopped to top off our tanks with fuel before I crossed the Blue Water Bridge at Port Huron, Michigan. It was at the gas station that the boys and I parted company. My goal was to go basically non-stop across Canada to Niagara Falls, but Jason & Brian like to stop more often, so they decided to ride up into *the thumb*.

The route to Niagara Falls was clearly marked, so picking up 402 to 401 to 403 and finally the QEW (Queen Elizabeth Way) was done without an unscheduled side-trip. A bit more attention is needed when going the other direction since Port Huron and Sarnia are less visited than the falls. A quick note here: my mileage was actual miles and included side-trips and backtracking and may include routes you would not choose. Because of the summer showers the day before, all was fresh and clean. Blue skies were overhead and only to the south were clouds just above the horizon. Most of the day was a comfortable 65 degrees.

I have been to Canada many times, especially as a teenager. I lived close to Canada until I enlisted in the Marine Corps and moved away to begin what turned out to be a 23-year career. My mind was on the scenery, but the Canadian station on my radio got my attention when they forecasted temperatures in the single digits for the night. Since I was planning to be in my two-man tent in upstate New York that night, the temperature was of interest to me. It didn't take me long to realize they were talking Celsius, not Fahrenheit.

Though I crossed back into the U.S. at Niagara Falls using 420 off of the QEW, it would be shorter using 405 off of the QEW to cross at the bridge a few miles north of the falls. That northern bridge puts the rider directly onto New York's 104 (SR104), which is the road I took for the next 188 miles. (As is common in the trucking industry, I'll refer to State Routes with "SR" before the number highway.) Northeast of the falls just off SR104 (one block south) on the Tuscarora Indian Reservation near Model City, I found Smokin Joe's gas to be 10-18 cents cheaper. One local lady said it was cheaper because there was an exemption of some taxes.

Just as the office was closing at 9:30 pm, I was checking into the KOA at Natural Bridge, New York. As the only one in the tent area, I had my choice of sites. The excitement of the first day seemed to make the first 465 miles go by too quickly.

Day One Summary:
11:15 hours, 465 miles, tent at KOA Natural Bridge, NY.

The last I remember of my first day was 11:15 pm in my sleeping bag. The first I remembered of my second day was an uneasy sleep the first night. I was up by 5:20 am and started my second day of riding at 6:15 am. It was cool and damp enough to wear the tight down coat I received from a sister-in-law when my nephew outgrew it. Over that warm coat, I wore my red GWRRA (Gold Wing Road Riders Association) Michigan, Chapter A jacket.

I hadn't gone far when I stopped for breakfast in Harrisville at the Hunter's View. My breakfast of two eggs, home fries, and two slices of toast, made of homemade bread, was only $1.95, so I figured I could afford another $1 for a very large orange juice. Was it my imagination, or was it freshly squeezed? The tip I got from Mike Jarosz while on a motorcycle trip years earlier was to eat at non-chain, non-franchised, local mom & pop restaurants. That had proved to be good advice in the past, so I intended to do more of that while on this trip.

While passing through Lake Placid, which was the site of the 1932 & 1980 Olympic Winter Games, I found the trailhead for the climb to Mt. Marcy begin at the Adirondack/ Adirondak Loj (pronounced Lodge). There was a $7 fee for parking. The road sign that leads to the lodge is: "Adiron*dack* Loj Rd," and the sign at the corner points to the "Adiron*dak* Loj," so I guess you take your pick at how you spell it, and you're correct either way, or are you wrong either way?

Mt. Marcy was named after three-term Governor William Learned Marcy, who had almost continuously held one public office or another for nearly 50 years. Marcy never climbed the summit that bears his name and may have only glanced at it from a relatively comfortable spot along Lake Champlain, many miles away. He was born in Southbridge, Massachusetts on December 12, 1786. As the son of a prosperous farmer, he received a solid education at Leicester Academy, then Brown University, where he graduated in 1808. When he settled in Troy, he took up the study of law and was admitted to the New York bar in 1811. At the outbreak of the War of 1812, he joined the New York 155th Regiment. Following the war, he married, and established a legal practice in Troy. His first political appointment was as city recorder of Troy. It was unusual then, and even more so now, to have a landmark named after some-one while they are still alive, but Mt. Marcy was named before his death, and, in fact, while he was sitting as governor. One might question his modesty.

While spending time at the Loj, I discovered that Mt. Marcy is within the Adirondak Park, which is comprised of more than 6,000,000 acres and is the largest park in the contiguous U.S. It is the largest wilderness area east of the Mississippi. With about 60 percent of the park privately owned, it has a unique mixture of public and private lands. Although used occasionally by the Indians as a hunting ground, this area remained unexplored and unsettled until the 1800s. Logging and mining were done in the 19th century. All too often the land was cleared of its valuable natural resources and then allowed to revert to the state for back taxes. Verplanck Colvin surveyed and explored much of the area and suggested the formation of the Adirondak Park to preserve the lands. In 1885 the Adirondack Forest Reserve was created so the public lands would be forever kept as wild forestlands.

In 1892 the Adirondack Park was established, which included the Adirondack Forest Reserve and the private lands, yet logging continued. Recreational use of the Adirondack increased during the late 1800s and early 1900s. Even as recently as 1971, the Adirondack Park Agency was established to encourage wise land use planning for the park.

One of the park rangers told me that four separate helicopter rescues were required along the trails around Mt. Marcy on Saturday, July 6th, 1996. As with many holiday weekends, inexperienced and/or ill-equipped hikers make their ways to the trails. It's becoming a significant problem. Consider for a moment who should pay for the helicopter, pilot, etc.

Spending a few hours around the Loj reading material and listening to rangers answer visitor's questions was a valuable introduction to hiking. CAUTION would summarize most of what I gleaned, but here is one specific: Cotton is about the worst clothing material for hiking because it takes too long to dry when wet. One report I picked up along the way stated that wet cotton clothes can cause loss of body heat as much as 17 times faster than just bare skin. This is something good to remember. Wear it when it's hot and you're on a bike, but not while on a hike, especially if you get caught in a rainstorm and the temperature also drops several degrees. Wool is a much better material for hiking because it helps retain body heat even if wet.

I had arrived too late to make a safe hike to the summit, so I hiked to Marcy Dam, which takes about 45 minutes, but I was gone almost two hours. There are also many other hikes from which to choose. A hike to the summit is a strenuous hike of 7.4 miles south from the parking lot on the Van Hoevenburg Trail, which is marked with blue markers. For the average hiker, this is a long, arduous day, but I met some boy scouts who had made the hike up, without packs and returned to the Loj by early afternoon.

Tim Reese, a newspaper photographer from Syracuse, New York, had started up the trail toward the Dam just ahead of me, so after I signed the ranger's log, I hustled up the trail to catch him. It was Tim who told me how to pronounce Loj (lodge), and he believed that it was Roosevelt who wanted to have things spelled the way they sound. This desire stuck at the Loj.

I also spent some time talking with a professor from Toronto, Canada, who was hiking up as I returned. Arnd was just enjoying nature, and I would not consider him a hiker. I also was not a hiker yet, but hoped I would get some experience during the next six weeks.

If I were going to camp near Mt. Marcy, I would consider Whispering Pines Campground, which is about three miles east of Adirondack Loj Rd. on SR73. It provides a choice of cabins—primitive and self-contained.

Route:

From Meade, MI (about 30 miles northeast of Detroit, near New Haven). East on 26 Mile Road to I-94 through Pt. Huron to Canada (toll: $1.50). 402, 401, 403 & QEW to Niagara Falls (235)*. (toll: $1.00) SR104 through Oswego. SR104B (and SR3) to Pulaski. US11 to Watertown. SR3 to Saranac Lake (565). SR86 to Lake Placid (571). SR73 to a junction with a sign indicating the route to Adirondak Loj on the right. Turn right (S) and proceed to the parking area near the Campers and Hikers Building (576).

* **Note:** The number in parentheses following a location was my trip odometer from the previous highpoint, or in this case, from home.

#02

Mount Mansfield, Vermont
(4,393 feet)

Blazes & Cairns.

I LEFT MT. MARCY AT 1 pm, crossed from New York into Vermont by car ferry ($3.75) at 2:15 pm on July 8th, hoping to have better luck on my visit to Mt. Mansfield than did fellow Highpointer Rick Peterson on his first visit. Rick endured fog for his first visit, so he returned a second time, when it was clear enough to make out individual buildings of Montreal. If I was going to keep to my schedule, I couldn't return during this trip.

Soon after rolling off the car ferry into Vermont, my attention was drawn off the road to my right, to a large black bear straddling a motorcycle in the middle of a garden. "That's what can happen to me on these curvy roads if I don't pay attention," I thought. He didn't seem hurt (he was stuffed), so after snapping a picture, I was on my way again.

Arriving at the Stowe Toll Road at 4:50 pm and paying $7 allowed me to use the road to the Summit Station. The bike was parked by 5:05 pm, and I embarked on foot for the easy Class 1 hike of about 1.4 miles.

Summit hikes are given a subjective class to advise the hiker of the degree of difficulty. The classes are:

DRIVE-UP: A motorcycle can be driven to the immediate vicinity.

CLASS 1: A hike on trails or easy cross-country, which can be done with your hands in your pockets. I recommend that you be in very good physical condition for some long class 1 hikes, especially if there is a significant gain in elevation. Some are not suitable for a Sunday afternoon stroll, but some are.

CLASS 2: Rough cross country hiking which may include boulder hopping and use of hands for balance. This is not for the typical couch potato.

CLASS 3: Handholds are necessary for climbing. Rope belays recommended, and I would discourage any attempt without training.

CLASS 4: Most difficult climbing with considerable travel on glaciers or snowfields. Ropes are required. This is only for the most serious hiker with good training and all of the proper gear.

A large sign near the Summit Station provided help for this "soon-to-be" hiker. I had heard of blazes and cairns, but it wasn't until I read that sign that I understood what they are. Blazes are painted rectangles about 3" x 6" and mark the footpath along the trail. Cairns (rock piles) also mark the trail to help guide the hiker in poor weather/visibility. Disturbing these trail markings may cause subsequent hikers significant problems. Please don't alter any blazes or cairns; lives may be at stake!

Along the trail, a plaque dated 1980 declared: "Mt. Mansfield Natural Area has been designated a national natural landmark." Although it was cloudy, I could see for several miles. I reached the benchmark at 5:50 pm, which is located on the chin of the mountain range that resembles the profile of a man's face looking heavenward.

What a rush! It was not the easy stroll along the path to the summit that had my knees knocking and my heart pounding.

Standing on the summit, all alone, near the end of my second day, was like crossing the threshold, 30 years earlier, with Jeri in my arms. This trip actually began about 30 hours earlier, but it was then that I knew I was not dreaming (again). I was actually on the trip that had beckoned me for two years.

Returning from the summit to the parking lot provided a totally different view. Instead of looking uphill toward a rocky summit, I was looking down on Vermont's inhabited countryside. I can only imagine that my mountain top experience was something like the feeling my Mom had in about 1947 when she authored her only poem, except that her experience was more spiritual.

I was just two or three years old, with four older brothers and one older sister. Mom was getting the family ready to attend special meetings at church one evening where the emphasis was visitation and inviting others to attend church to meet Jesus. Some details were still as clear as day as Mom recently recounted preparing a kidney bean stew for supper. Although my older brothers were often very helpful, it was still no small task for Mom and Dad to get a family of eight fed and dressed to go to church. Those were the days when more families got dressed up and went to church together.

As Mom brought supper to the table, the bowl broke and the kidney bean stew spilled over the table. There was no microwave to quickly do another meal, no McDonalds, Burger King, or Taco Bell, even if they had the money to feed eight. "Disappointment" can hardly paint the picture.

At the church evening service, with emphasis on visitation, Mom said that she felt like crying. Looking up seemed to help keep tears from her eyes, but she didn't escape the challenge. She said it was hard enough to just get her own family fed and ready for church each week when things went well. Did God expect more? The only poem Mom authored had its start that evening. The words came the next day.

Mountain Top Experience
by Eunice J. Mick

I dwelt one day upon a mountain.
I met my Master there.
I knew the comfort of His blessing.
I vowed I'd serve Him anywhere.

"Anywhere?" my Master queried.
"Look down yonder in the Vale.
They too would like to reach this summit.
Go, and bring them here to dwell."

So I turned and left my Master
Knowing He was waiting there;
And I sought to lift up others
By kindly deeds, by word, and prayer.

Dear friend, if you have missed that summit
Look up, the Master's waiting there.
Come dwell a while in His Sweet Presence
Then go, and with another share.

I must needs go down more often
For there are many to be won.
But OH! The joy of that fair morning
When He reaches forth and says "Well Done."

Once you have had a mountaintop experience, you too will understand the pleasure of enjoying what is waiting at the summit and will likely want others to experience the summits. Hopefully this book will encourage you to visit the state summits just as Mom's poem has been an encouragement for me to "...dwell a while in His Sweet Presence then go, and with another share."

Route:

From Mt. Marcy in NY: SR73 through Keene. SR9N to Elizabethtown (29). US-9 through Lewis (35) then east to Essex (47). Toll Ferry ($3.75) to VT. SR5F (Church Hill Rd, Hinesburg Rd, and more) through Charlotte, Hinesburg and Richmond. US2 to SR100 just before Waterbury. SR100 through Colbyville (82) to SR108 to Stowe Auto Rd (97). Toll ($7) to proceed to the Summit Station parking lot (102).

#03

Mount Washington, New Hampshire

(6,288 feet)

Who are the savages?

T HE RADIO STATIONS WERE forecasting rain through the night. The bike was already dirty, so I didn't mind riding in the rain, but the anticipation of setting up the tent in the rain provided very little excitement. Since the rain started soon after leaving Mt. Mansfield, I settled down for the night at a motel in Lancaster, New Hampshire, just 86 miles from the summit station.

While nosing around the lobby of the motel the next morning and enjoying some hot chocolate with my continental breakfast, I met Joseph and Julia Imre from Ottawa, Canada, who were traveling with their grandson Joe. It was still raining and was expected to continue all day. Joseph asked about traveling in the rain on a motorcycle, and I was unprepared to respond the way I had prayed. As a member of the CMA (Christian Motorcyclists Association), I had prayed that I would have opportunities to earn the right to share Jesus with as many people as possible. Back in my room I had a pocket size tract titled "Everything You Ever Wanted to Know About A

Motorcyclist...But Were Afraid to Ask." That tract, after explaining that most of us are friendly folks and why some motorcyclists wear leather, answers the question I had just been asked: "What do you do if it rains?"

We had a pleasant exchange of questions during breakfast and then returned to our rooms. It wasn't until later that I understood Joseph's interest in the details about my book. He asked if I had chosen a publisher and commented about the importance of selecting the right one. As I finished packing, Joseph knocked on my door.

Joseph was born in Budapest, Hungary, and has written several short novels and poems in his mother tongue. After moving to Canada, he wrote several political essays and study papers. Standing outside, sheltered from the rain by the building's eve, he held out a copy of *Triton*, the second book he had published in English. Inside he had written "To Jim, Happy Motoring" above his autograph. *Triton* is fiction and takes the reader to the future, a place of beauty, innocence and peace. The book has a touch of dreams, a touch of Jules Verne, and more than just a touch of promise. When he came to my room with his gift, I had a second chance to share the tract with the Imres, and I did, then we said our farewells. After I watched them leave the parking lot of the motel, I finished packing and was on the road just a few miles behind them.

The weather on the morning of July 9th as I approached the auto road to Mt. Washington's summit was not bad. The rain had decreased and no longer required rain gear.

Mt. Washington is part of a range with namesakes for nearly a dozen presidents, including Mt. Pierce, named after President Franklin Pierce, but also called Mt. Clinton. Folks around here are proud that two U.S. Presidents visited the summit of Mt. Washington during their terms of office: Ulysses S. Grant on August 27, 1869, and Rutherford B. Hayes on August 20, 1877. Franklin Pierce was New Hampshire's only native son to be elected president, but completed his term of office before he made a trip to the summit.

Highpointer Mike Bromberg, from Mason, New Hampshire, has seen Gold Wings on the summit and highly recommended actually going all the way to the highpoints that are short day hikes, so that was my goal during this trip. I would not attempt summits that others recommended I should not do or if I felt the risk was more than I was willing to accept.

I wanted to get a picture of our Wing on the summit, but Mt. Washington has fog & clouds 300 days per year and has the reputation for having the world's worst weather. Beyond reputation, it does have winds above 75 mph more than 100 days per year. The highest wind velocity in the world was recorded on Mt. Washington, April 12, 1934, when the instrument broke recording winds of 231 mph. The coldest temperature recorded was minus 47 degrees farenheit in January 1934, and the summit gets snowstorms every month of the year with about 255 inches annually. The maximum snowfall was more than 47 feet in the 1968-69 season. Even though August held the highest temperature of 72 degrees farenheit, I opted to pay $20 for the round-trip with the Glen & Mt. Washington Stage Company in the comfort of the specially equipped GMC van. I discovered it to be a wise decision and reached the summit at 10:05 am.

The pathway we traveled to the summit was known as the Mt. Washington Carriage Road when it first opened to the public back in 1861. It remains private property, but is called the auto road and serves one primary purpose of allowing visitors to the summit. The base of the road is about 1600 feet. For those who know trees, you are correct in assuming that hardwood trees abound at the base. Along the drive, the hardwoods give way to pine, then ash, and decrease in size until no trees exist before reaching the summit. Eight miles up the 12 percent grade, on a road that is 70 percent paved, travelers find themselves in a different world at 6,288 feet. The summit is staffed year round, but the last overnight accommodations for guests stood until 1962.

In earlier years, specially built horsedrawn mountain

wagons provided rides to the summit. Six-horse teams were changed halfway up, and the evidence of their history remains today—the van driver is still referred to as your stage driver. Though the first automobile to the summit of Mt. Washington was a Stanley Steamer on August 31, 1899, it wasn't until 1916 that automobiles replaced the horsedrawn wagons.

As it was in the early days when visitors were allowed to take their own buckboards and carriages to the summit, today's travelers may take themselves or enjoy a guided tour in a comfortable GMC van while a knowledgeable stage driver tells about the mountain's legends and lore. Driving your own vehicle affords you the opportunity to linger at any of the scenic vistas along the route. A free audio tour on cassette is available for those who choose to do their own driving but still want to hear a few classic stories about Mt. Washington's history, geography, climate, and wildlife. The observatory resource center at the summit is free while the museum costs $1.

About a dozen hiking trails to the summit are maintained for those choosing to make the hike. This hike is not to be taken without preparation since this mountain has claimed more lives than any other in the country, second only in the world to Mt. Everest, which only recently took the lead. Many hikers unprepared for the weather changes have learned valuable lessons on these slopes. Unfortunately, too many have paid with their lives. As of my visit, 123 had died on Mt. Washington, but only two fatalities were on the road. The following words of Edward Whymper are posted in the Observatory: "There have been joys too great to describe in words, and there have been griefs upon which I have not dared to dwell, and with these in mind I say: Climb if you will, but remember that courage and strength are not without prudence...Do nothing in haste, look well to each step, and from the beginning think what may be the end."

Three races to the summit are held each year. June 21st, 1997, was the 37th foot race, which is limited to 1000 runners. Daniel Kihara established a new record time of 58 minutes and 21 seconds in 1996, which remained for at least four years. The biggest race is the Auto Climb to the Clouds, with a record time of six minutes and 45 seconds set in 1995 by Paul Choiniere, but that was broken in 1998 by Frank Sprongl with a time of just under six minutes and 42 seconds. In late August is the bicycle race, which used to allow as many as 3-4,000 entries. That has recently been limited to about 600 entries. When I visited, the 17-year record of Dale Stetina was 57 minutes and 41 seconds. About a month after my visit, Tyler Hamilton set a new record of 51 minutes and 55 seconds and then broke his own record again in 1999 with a time of 50 minutes and 21 seconds. As one would expect, there have been several accidents during races, but to my surprise, none have included very bad injuries.

According to the *A. M. C. White Mountain Guide*, compiled and edited by Gene Daniell and Jon Burroughs, the Crawford Path, which runs from near the highest point in Crawford Notch to the summit of Mt. Washington, is considered to be the oldest footpath in America that has been continuously maintained. Abel and his son Ethan Crawford cut the first section of the path in 1819. In 1840 Thomas Crawford, another son of Abel, converted it into a bridle path. Nathaniel T. P. Davis, a son-in-law of Abel, constructed the longest bridle path in 1845, which became impassable within ten years and eventually ceased existence until the Appalachian Mountain Club reopened it as a foot trail in 1910.

How America ended up with the land we now call the United States has been written about in many books, but I found the following account to help me answer the question: "Who are the savages?"

In 1854 President Franklin Pierce made an offer to buy/trade for a large area of Indian land. When I read the reply of Chief Sealth of the Duamish Tribe, it changed the picture I had of the Indians whom our forefathers encountered. The chief asked several questions about how someone could buy or sell the sky and warmth of the land, the freshness of the air, and the sparkle of the water. He went on to illustrate the difference between how white men and Indians looked at the earth. The chief spoke of the earth as the mother of the red man. He also charged the Great Chief in Washington to teach his children that the rivers are brothers to all of us. But what I was most amused about was the numerous times the chief said that he was a savage and did not understand the white man's attitude about the earth. Over the years since Chief Sealth, the white man has illustrated that we may in fact be the savages and don't understand how to treat and care for this earth.

Mt. Washington is located in the northern White Mountains, which is the Moose Capital of New Hampshire. Watch for New Hampshire's most famous resident during moose tours, which leave daily in mid-June through foliage season, from the Gorham information booth (reservations strongly suggested).

According to the official *New Hampshire Guidebook* of 1996-97, trains have played an important part in popularizing the White Mountains as a destination. In 1869 the Boston, Concord & Montreal Railroad received authorization to build a branch line to the region. That same year, the Mt. Washington Cog Railway was completed, and the original "Little Engine That Could" first reached the summit of Mt. Washington on July 3. Similar coal-fired steam engines are still in use today and make journeys on "the railway to the moon." They consume one ton of coal and 1,000 gallons of water for each three-hour round-trip excursion along the second steepest railway track in the world. The White Mountain branch reached Twin Mountain in 1873, Fabyan's in 1874, and connected with the Mt. Washington Cog Railway in 1876. The Notch Train carries passengers through Crawford Notch and past some of the finest natural scenery in the entire Northeast. The Valley Train offers an excursion to Conway and Bartlett.

An Englishman named Darby Field is generally believed to be the first white person to have climbed the mountain in 1642. To make the climb, he recruited two Abenaki Indians to guide him. At the summit, he reportedly stuffed his pockets with quartz crystals, thinking they might be valuable gems.

In addition to some of the presidents of the U.S. visiting the summit, other famous people have as well. For example, Henry David Thoreau visited the peak in 1858. But many more people make the journey and are pleased they did 250,000 tourists annually. (50,000 by foot, 150,000 by car, and 50,000 by cog).

One of the unique things about Mt. Washington is the degree to which man has associated himself with it. From the day in 1642 when Darby Field, with his Indian guides, finally reached the summit of the Crystal Hills in a forlorn search for precious gems, interest in the White Mountains has grown steadily. The first few pioneers and adventurers penetrated the wilderness on horseback or by coach and rested at crude hostels. They were followed in time by the railroads, which brought trainloads of visitors and created pressure for the development of the areas highest peak. In the mid-19th century, bridle paths gave way to the Carriage Road and the Cog Railway, and elegant hotels catering to hundreds every night replaced surrounding inns. Soon, the summit of Mt. Washington also sported a luxury motel with its own orchestra. A weather observatory, a large survey tower, numerous barns, sheds, ticket and telegraph offices, and even a newspaper print shop surrounded it!

Now the summit is a state park, a tiny island within the White Mountain National Forest. Though fire destroyed the City Among the Clouds in 1908, another community has taken its place, centered in the Sherman Adams Building, a modern facility designed to serve the visiting public.

Because of the weather, only occasionally is it possible to look from the summit into Maine, Vermont, Massachusetts, New York and Canada. In 1524, Giovanni da Verrazano was the first to report seeing Mt. Washington, which native Americans called *Agiocochook*, from the waters off Portsmouth, so on a clear day a visitor should be able to see a sliver of the Atlantic Ocean from its summit.

Some of the Chronology:

First known sighting by a European (Verrazano)	1524
First climbed by a European (Darby Field)	1642
First scientific expedition (Belknap)	1784
First trail to the summit	1819
First bridle path	1840
Stone summit inn built	1852
Tip-Top House built (still standing)	1853
Carriage Road opened after six years of work	1861
Cog Railway open after four years of work	1869
S. Signal Corps began weather observatory	1871
Two-and-a-half-story Summit House built	1873
First printing of newspaper, *Among the Clouds*	1877
Great fire leveled most of summit community	1908
Summit House rebuilt on smaller scale	1915
Mt. Washington Observatory founded	1932
First Mt. Washington Observatory building	1937
Yankee Network FM Station built	1941
WMTW-TV Station built	1954
State of NH purchased summit	1964
Mt. Washington Museum opened	1973

The geology of Mt. Washington is explained by the museum, but left me with more questions than answers. For example, they claim "...the resistant bedrock of which this peak is composed had humble beginnings as a mixture of sand and mud, deposited in the ancestral Atlantic Ocean, some 400,000,000 years ago..." I recalled an announcement by some scientists in the late '70s that the sun may be shrinking and wondered how big the sun would have been if our solar system is really that old. Would a larger sun be hotter and cause more gravitational pull on our planets? Recalling some basic physics, it seems that gravity has something to do with body mass (size) and distance apart. The larger the objects, the greater the force needed to pull them together. My point:

we need not accept everything we read or hear, so I didn't accept that as the beginning of Mt. Washington.

Route:

From Mt. Mansfield in VT: Out the Stowe Auto Rd to SR108 to Stowe. SR100 to Morrisville. SR15A to SR15 to US-2 through Lancaster NH (86) to Gorham. SR16 to Mt. Washington Auto Road to the Summit (116).

Sidetrips:

If you like cassette tours, try the 2 1/2-hour, 95-mile loop through some of the most scenic sections of New Hampshire. Hear the amazing history, legends, cures and lore of the region. Identify your favorite spots, attractions and activities, note them on the exclusive tour map, then finalize your plans after taking the tour on your own motorcycle, or ride their coach, and leave the driving to them. You might also consider renting or purchasing a Central Notch tour kit at local retail outlets or at the Privatours Cassette tour office on Rt. 16 in Conway.

If you're in the Lancaster area on Sunday, you may want to enjoy a pancake breakfast served Memorial Day through Columbus Day on Sundays from 7:00 am until noon at Christie's Maple Farm. This is an authentic working sugar-house with majestic views and educational tours with emphasis on samples.

Whether you have a fascination with covered bridges, New Hampshire is a place to begin or expand that interest. The Cornish-Windsor covered bridge, just north of Claremont, is touted as the longest covered bridge in the U.S. New Hampshire's covered bridges are often a testament to the tenacity of the state's citizens. The current Bath Bridge is the fifth bridge to stand on its site. Three of the first four were destroyed by floods, while the other was destroyed by fire. The nearby Swiftwater Bridge is the fourth bridge on its site.

If time allows and you enjoy curves and hills, try a visit along a National Scenic Byway, the Kancamagus Highway. This is the only National Scenic Byway in New England. It climbs to nearly 3,000 feet as it winds through the 780,000-acre White Mountain National Forest from the Pemigewasset River in Lincoln to the town of Conway. The original route was started in 1837, which means it's not straight. It wasn't until 1959 that it opened, but paving wasn't completed until 1964. Along the way are dramatic views, national forest campgrounds, picnic spots, swimming areas, waterfalls, and many hiking trails.

#04

Mount Katahdin, Maine
(5,267 feet)

Some people don't like motorcycles.

T HERE WERE MANY times during this venture when I wished others were along to share the enjoyment of my quest, but the trip from Mt. Washington to Mt. Katahdin was not one of those. The ride was cold and wet most of the way to Baxter State Park. After a long day in almost constant rain, I checked into a motel for the night in Millinocket before continuing to the park.

Mt. Katahdin (Abenakis Indian word for greatest mountain) is approximately 20 miles northwest of Millinocket and is within the Baxter State Park. It is the northern terminus of the famous 2,025-mile Appalachian Trail that was completed in 1937. The highest point on Mt. Katahdin is named Baxter Peak and is the first place the sun hits the continental U.S. on a clear morning.

Former Governor Percival Baxter had been unable to convince the Maine legislature that preservation of Katahdin and its environment was a worthy public goal, so he purchased the lands with his own money and donated them to the state through 28 deeds over a 32-year period. One term of acceptance of his gift was that the state agree to maintain the park as a wilderness area. That explains why there are no telephones or piped water and only a few narrow gravel roads. He also required that motorcycles not be allowed to enter the park. That restriction would have only been a slight problem for me on this trip if things had gone as planned.

There may be no logical reason I felt as I did upon arriving at the Togue Pond entrance to Baxter State Park. Maybe it had something to do with spending a long day on a motorcycle in almost constant rain. I knew from several sources that motorcycles are not allowed in the park and the director's reply to my request for a special permit made it clear that his hands were tied. So why did I feel revenge was the next step? That's not like me! I know that most rules are for our benefit.

During the several mile ride back to Millinocket, thoughts raced through my mind. Did the former governor have a bad experience with motorcyclists? Was he trying to limit vehicle travel to the roads and didn't trust motorcyclists to obey rules? (He couldn't have guessed that touring motorcycles as we have today are less likely to go off the road than the family sedan, or today's ever more popular sport utility vehicle.) Maybe it was a restriction because he thought motorcycles are noisy, but, in fact, the noise of the Jeep Grand Cherokee entering the park as I was leaving drowned out the whisper of our Wing. In an effort to provide a peaceful wilderness experience, they do restrict radio use to a volume that others can't hear.

I can understand if Mr. Baxter's desire was to preserve its wilderness character—free of chain saws and clear-cuts—but the presence of motorcycles in the park does not in itself change the character, except to beautify it while there. There are a few cabins and bunkhouses, but evidently that's considered wilderness.

Since the restriction is not "motorcyclists," we can't claim discrimination, but I now have a better idea how the Negroes must have felt a few years ago when told they had to go to the back of the bus or couldn't use the white man's restroom.

I was seriously considering getting a copy of the deeds to

see the verbiage of what stipulations he set. I have no doubt he didn't like motorcycles and did want people to experience nature. No telephones, but would he object to cellular phones? Whether it was Mr. Baxter's intent, visitors are asked to not use their cell phones except in an emergency. No piped water, but why not restrict the use of outside water that was brought in? Did he just want people to see the wilderness and not have to experience it? Bring chlorinated water, bug spray, ambulances and helicopters to rescue people when they have an accident, etc. Where's the wilderness experience? Marked trails? Improved hiking equipment? Do you see where my mind was going?

Maybe part of the anger was that the director of the park had offered to meet me at the Togue Pond entrance to Baxter State Park. I could leave my motorcycle at the entrance and he would arrange a ride anywhere in the park so I could make my hike. I had accepted his offer and sent a postcard on July 1 about when I planned to arrive. I arrived a couple of hours early but figured the ranger at the entrance would have expected me. The ranger at the gate said the director was giving a class at the time I arrived and she was given no information about my arrival.

Correspondence back and forth had been slow between the park director and me before I left home. His last letter, received at home some time after my visit, stated that he had received my acceptance to his offer six days after I had been at the park. Because of the bad weather, I would not have attempted a climb, but I did want to get a better view and picture of the summit.

Katahdin: A Guide to Baxter State Park by Stephen Clark was highly recommended as a source of information on access routes, trails and park history, but it was difficult to get excited about a place where I was not allowed to take our Gold Wing.

Although Mt. Katahdin is a Class 1 hike (hands in pocket), the first newspaper article I read on it was about Jeffery Rubin, an experienced hiker, who lost his life attempting to climb it. I took three lessons from the article that were not necessarily the intentions of the author: 1) don't hike alone; 2) don't be pushed by a schedule; and 3) not all Class 1 highpoints are easy to climb.

When they found Mr. Rubin, he had several abrasions, his jacket appeared to be placed so that others would be helped to find him, etc. Maybe he recognized early signs of hypothermia: sleepiness, lethargy, just wanting to lie down, surprisingly not feeling very cold. He was alone and trying to complete the hike before meeting someone in another state. He may have pushed the envelope instead of accepting the fact that conditions were not good for the challenge. Conditions dictate everything; in his case, bad weather should have caused him to back off on that day.

Pamola has been blamed for the weather many find at Mt. Katahdin. According to native Abenaki Indian lore, *Pamola*, a vengeful Indian god—part giant bird, part moose, part human—uses his power over the elements to keep man off the summit of Katahdin. Many early explorers, including Henry David Thoreau, reported that Indian guides were extremely reluctant to venture to the top. According to the September 23, 1996 *New Yorker*, Mr. Thoreau climbed Mt. Katahdin on September 7 and 8, 1846 and described it as "something savage and awful." That was 12 years before he made it to the summit of Mt. Washington. I don't know how he compared the two.

During the two-hour descent from a failed attempt, D. C. Denison and his 10-year-old son Tom were chewing over their defeat. Mr. Denison's theory was that it is presumptuous to assume that they could climb Katahdin on the one Saturday that was convenient for them. Climbers must be willing to devote a few dates to the project, so they can wait for just the right conditions. Tom thought that *Pamola* got angry because of a gum wrapper he had seen under a rock along the trail.

Before this six-week trip began, I listened to a hiker telling that his group had given up on one climb when they were within 100 feet of the summit of another highpoint. Before I knew better, I thought it a shame to not leave the injured hiker, complete the climb and pick him up on their way down. I have become aware that a schedule can push us beyond safety and fun. Some Highpointers have made several attempts at the more difficult climbs—spending weeks at different elevations, waiting for weather to clear — only to call it off without making it to the top.

This might be a good place to talk a little about locating and measuring highpoints. According to Third Quarter *1995 A to Z Newsletter*, in August 1874, University of Maine (UM) professor Merritt Caldwell Fernald used barometers to measure Mt. Katahdin at 5,215.5 feet (plus or minus 4.2 feet). According to Fernald's original report, his party made six or seven trips to the summit on August 15, 17, and 18, 1874. They carried mercury barometers and recorded changes in atmospheric pressure from the bottom to the summit. Fernald then calculated the altitude by taking the average of the measurements.

Professor Fernald's grandson John A. Pierce was a part of a recent UM team that checked that figure using satellites, signals and computers in 1993. A satellite receiver and antenna system was carefully placed on the highest point. The receiver captured signals from four or five Global Positioning System satellites during a two-hour period. 20 miles away at a base station in Millinocket, at a federal geodetic altitude marker, another receiver was receiving signals. The series of signals from the satellites provided information to be analyzed using geometrical calculations. Results: 5,271.13 feet (plus or minus three inches). But was it official? Not that quickly.

In 1941 the peak's altitude was calculated by the USGS using a process called triangulation — same basic idea of the satellites. It came up with 5,267 feet. Whether it is actually 5,271 or 5,267 or even something else might not matter much unless another place in the state was close to that. Since there needs to be one authority, most are satisfied with waiting for the USGS to make it official.

ROUTE:

From Mt. Washington in NH: Mt. Washington Auto Rd to SR16 to Gorham. US-2 to Maine. US2 through Farmington Falls to Skowhegan. SR150 to Guilford. SR16 to Milo. SR11 to Millinocket then northwest out of town to Baxter State Park (228).

#05

Jerimoth Hill, Rhode Island
(812 feet)

Some people don't like hikers.

As I PREPARED TO leave the motel in Millinocket, the morning weather reports promised expectations for a much-improved day. The Wing was dirty from too many miles of riding in the rain, and though the roads were still wet and a light rain was falling when I left, I chose to stow my rain gear. The aerodynamics of the Gold Wing are good at deflecting light rain away from the rider, so I was able to stay quite dry while moving. I stopped for fuel and breakfast right away to allow a little more time for the storm front to pass. I must have chased the weather southward because I ended up riding in and out of light rains for the first 100 miles.

While planning for this six-week trip, I made several commitments. One of the things I decided to do was to stop and offer help to every motorist I saw along the road. All too often, I am too busy or in too much of a rush to stop. I wanted to make this trip different. That morning I had my first of several opportunities to see if I would follow through with my commitment. I offered help to two separate motorists along I-95 between 8 and 9 am. Neither of them needed my help, so I continued.

By 2:35 pm, with partly sunny skies, the temperature was up to 80 degrees, so my long sleeve cotton GWRRA, Michigan, Chapter A shirt was perfect. By 5:30 pm, I had traveled 408 miles and arrived at the road sign for Jerimoth Hill.

A couple of recent explorers were Lauri Alkins and her husband. They started aiming for Americas highpoints in Rhode Island. They were driving along admiring the foliage one cool October day that was filled with the smell of earth and leaves. Her husband saw the sign first: *Jerimoth Hill, Highest Point in Rhode Island, 812 feet,* so he pulled off to the side of the road. Some folks get started as Highpointers just that quickly.

As with all the highpoints, I had collected information on Jerimoth Hill for two years preceding this trip. I learned that Henry Richardson owns about five acres between the road sign and Jerimoth Hill, which includes an access road, but he does not appreciate other people crossing his property to get to the highpoint. In an effort to respect Mr. Richardsons wishes, at the Highpointer s Konvention in 1994 (Highpointers have Konventions rather than conventions Jack (AKA Jakk) Longacre started that), a motion was passed to recognize the sign along the edge of the highway as the official highpoint, but that did not keep everyone off of his property. According to the July 19, 1996 issue of *The Wall Street Journal,* Mr. Richardson said: The last time somebody got on (my land), I threatened to break their camera equipment.

Thanks to horseman Jim Duffy, whose family, too, owns private property adjoining the hill, a southerly approach on Duffy s property was a pleasant way to go for Highpointer Bob Greenawalt in April 1996 as reported in the Third Quarter 1996 *A to Z Newsletter.* Mr. Duffy (Pine Ridge Farm II, 116 East Killingly Road, just south of the hill) allowed Bob access over one of his horse trails off of highway 101, about 228 feet east of the Jerimoth Hill sign.

Nick Williams, also a Highpointer, reported in the same newsletter of 1996 that he encountered some type of wild creature which chilled his very marrow. He described the bizarre animal as a dwarf hunchback bear standing upright, emitting unintelligible ramblings, and strangely enough, carrying a cellular phone! It said he was trespassing on private property, that it was tired of trespassers, and that it got so busy here on some weekends, that five to ten people would try to cross the private property to reach the promised land.

Another Highpointer, Bruce Marshall, reported in the *A to Z Newsletter* of the Fourth Quarter 1996 that a rage-filled Richardson, carrying a pistol, confronted him in the afternoon on August 26, 1996. While he did not point it at Marshall, he was definitely carrying the weapon. When Marshall got his camera out, Richardson hid behind a tree, so Bruce wasn't able to get a photo of him with the gun.

Highpointer Jeff Fisher went to Jerimoth Hill in October 1995, saw all the no trespassing signs, walked 50 yards down the road east, cut south when the neighbors dogs began barking, and said it was the scariest of the 27 highpoints he did in a three-week trip that month.

With these mixed messages collected before arriving at Jerimoth Hill, I wasn't afraid, but my preconceptions of the area were way off. I met Billy Stevens, who lives in a trailer with his wife, about 100 yards east of the Jerimoth Hill sign on SR 101/Hartford Pike. He offered to escort me through his property and over to the summit, which is located on the property of Brown University. Brown University has a right of way through Richardson's property, but it does not extend that right to others.

Several times Billy apologized for the underbrush, which had materialized since the last time he had been to the highpoint. He knew where we had to go, but he had to blaze a new trail along the way.

Because some highpoints are on, or require crossing, private property and situations change, it is extremely wise to be involved with the Highpointers Club. Subsequent to my visit, the club has been successful in establishing a few *open access dates* with the Richardsons. During the annual Konvention in Missouri during July 1999, the board of directors of the Highpointers Club voted to NOT recognize any completer who did not properly visit this highpoint. For recognition, Highpointers who claim Rhode Island after July 1999 must have visited the actual summit on an open access date or settle for the sign by the highway. Unfortunately for the Richardson family, not everyone who has a desire to visit the summit is a Highpointer or respects their right to privacy. If you intend to visit Rhode Island, please do so only on an access date arranged between the owners near the highpoint and the Highpointers Club. Access Dates are updated and posted at www.highpointers.com.

ROUTE:

From Mt. Katahdin in ME: Private Road to Millinocket. SR157 to Medway. I-95 past Augusta to I495 to Exit 11. US-202 through Sanford to NH. US-202 to SR125 through NH into MA to I-495. Exit 20 (SR85) to Milford. SR16 through Uxbridge. SR122 to SR98 to SR102 to SR101 then west to Jerimoth Hill (408).

#06

Mount Greylock, Massachusetts

(3,487 feet)

On a clear day you can see Florida.

AFTER LEAVING JERIMOTH Hill, I visited Jeff & Becky Garner in nearby Medway, Massachusetts. I first met Jeff in early 1985 when I reported for duty in Hawaii. Jeff was the Supply Officer of 3d Battalion, 3d Marines, and he quickly gained my trust. Our first computer and software was based on his recommendation.

Jeff and Becky became very special in my life when they visited me one Christmas Eve. While the Battalion was deployed to Okinawa, I was standing duty as Officer of the Day, and they brought a plate of snacks for me on that special day of the year.

Because I spent about half of my career in the Marine Corps as an enlisted man before my appointment as a Warrant Officer, I know what it is to man a post — often alone. The following version of an old Christmas favorite has special meaning to me and may for you or a friend also. It is one of a few keepsakes I brought back from Vietnam on a hard-to-read mimeographed copy that had been passed among Marines at Quang Tri. Its author is unknown.

'Twas the night before Christmas, with stars shining bright,
The sentry was walking to his left, then his right.
His rifle, it swung from his shoulder with ease,
His head kept alert from a chill in the breeze.

The troops were all nestled and warm in their racks,
While he stood his duty, his feet making tracks.
For he, in his helmet, with rifle at his side,
Had just settled down in that 24 to 4 stride.

Then what to the shock of the sentry appeared,
Was a little green sleigh pulled by camouflaged deer,
With a little old driver in dress blues and sword.
The sentry just stood there not saying a word.

He watched in amazement with eyes all aglow,
As the reindeer, in silence, pulled the sleigh low.
With a wink from the driver, a tip from his cover,
The sleigh, like a Huey, just pulled up and hovered.

The sentry was startled, bewitched, and in doubt,
But duty prevailed and these words rang out:

"Now wait just a minute - Halt, who goes there!?"
But the little man smiled, "You've nothing to fear,
For 'sure as it's Christmas, and sure as you're here,
I've stopped on my route just to bring you good Cheer!"

"For attention to duty while walking your post,
On this day of the year that we cherish the most,
Here in this place on this solemn occasion,
I thank you, Marine, on behalf of the nation!"

He saluted the sentry, with cut sharp and clear,
Then took up the reins as he called to his deer.

"On Belleau, on Iwo, on An-Hoa and Chosin,
On, you named, for places both hell-hot and frozen!"

And he called out once more as he sped out of sight,
"Merry Christmas Marine, carry on and good night!"

Although Jeri and I had not seen Jeff and Becky since 1987, we had exchanged letters at Christmas. When they found out I was going to be near them, they invited me to spend the night. So after Jerimoth Hill, I headed for Medway, where Jeff, carrying their four-month-old daughter out of the house, greeted me with a hug. He had been off that day (July 10th) for a minor surgery and it was a wonderful reunion — but too short since I was back on the road after breakfast the next morning.

The stay with Jeff and Becky would have been great even if the weather was bad, but the morning sunshine and a blue sky welcomed the new day. After breakfast, I took the parting photograph as Becky stood with Jeff who was holding their daughter. They were positioned behind our clean dark teal Gold Wing and in front of their dark teal minivan. No, I didn't choose dark teal because Jeff did—it just happened that way.

When you read that it was almost 10:30 am when I left, you'll understand that I had enjoyed the visit and found it difficult to say goodbye. It was almost 80 degrees and perfect for a scenic route - up and down, back and forth, through the hills and Gardner, where Jeff & Becky had previously lived.

Along SR2 (The Mohawk Trail) I offered help to a couple along the road who had two girls in the back seat. Their hood was up and he said they needed no help. He was letting the engine cool. It's hard to know whether he was too macho to ask for help, didn't like motorcyclists, or what. Either way, they all seemed fine, and I continued on my quest.

Mt. Greylock received only a small mention in the *Massachusetts GETAWAY Guide* of 1996-97, but where it is mentioned boasts of a higher elevation than recognized by the USGS. Whether it is 3,487 feet or 3,491 feet as claimed in all other brochures I found, it was well worth the trip, especially on a day with such great weather.

I approached from North Adams on a wonderful drive up a good blacktop road. A road crew was out doing repairs and cleanup, which must have been caused by the bad weather I had ridden through a couple days earlier. It was so bad that I almost turned back when I saw their sign, *ROAD CLOSED TO THRU TRAFFIC*, but when I talked to a worker, he said it would pose no problem for me and encouraged me to go on. He said I would enjoy the ride but should take it easy because of the debris on the road.

The last several miles before the summit reminded me of *Alice in Wonderland* when Alice followed the rabbit through the brush. The tree branches joined above and resembled a burrow with a paved road on the bottom.

At the summit parking lot, a couple had the hood of their minivan up with questioning looks on their faces. After I secured my helmet, I went over to offer help. The coolant in the overflow tank was unsettling. Evidently the heat of the engine was boiling the coolant in the block, which expanded and forced bubbles into the overflow tank. I suggested that if they start the engine and let it circulate some of the cooler water into the engine, it would likely stop. He did, and it did. They thanked me for giving them peace of mind that a tow truck was not necessary.

The Massachusetts War Memorial, with its 100 spiral stair steps, is on the highpoint, but there is no USGS benchmark. It was so clear the day I visited that I could literally see cars in Florida, where I had been about an hour earlier. A wooden weather observatory was constructed on the summit in 1841, which was replaced in 1889 with an iron tower that stood until 1933, when the current 90 foot granite tower was built. Just a few yards from the monument is the Bascom Lodge.

The Bascom Lodge is a rustic stone and wood lodge built by the Civilian Conservation Corps in the 1930s to provide accommodations for up to 36 hikers, vacationers, and nature enthusiasts. It is open throughout the riding season (mid-May to mid-October) and serves family-style breakfast and dinner that is guaranteed to satisfy the heartiest appetite. Reservations are required for lodging and meals. On the lighter side, a snack bar serves a variety of trail snacks, beverages, and sandwiches. You'll also find a trading post stocked with hiker supplies, maps, T-shirts, postcards, and guidebooks.

When you visit, I wish for you the same refreshing, clear, 72-degree day I had, as you enjoy what the summit has to offer. You'll find stone fireplaces, high ceilings with hand-cut oak beams, and a porch with large windows that provides an ideal atmosphere for dining, relaxing after a hike, or just enjoying the finest views in the Berkshires.

The AMC (Appalachian Mountain Club) has operated Bascom Lodge since 1982 in partnership with the Massachusetts Department of Environmental Management. Since 1876, the AMC has promoted the protection, enjoyment, and wise use of the mountains, rivers, and trails of the Northeast. Their 65,000 members, in 11 Chapters from Washington, D. C., to Maine offer a wide range of recreational opportunities from hiking to biking, rock climbing to canoeing.

A variety of educational programs and outdoor skills workshops are offered at both Bascom Lodge on the summit of Mt. Greylock and at the visitor center at the southern base of the mountain. The AMC is a nonprofit membership organization. Its programs and facilities are open to members and nonmembers alike.

A rockslide in 1990 exposed an impressive outcropping on Mt. Greylock's eastern slope. From Gould Road the exposed rock resembles an angry Indian profile. Local lore has it that it could be the Agawam Chief Greylock, reclaiming the mountain that bears his name.

ROUTE:

From Jerimoth Hill in RI: Since I stayed overnight in Medway, MA, I backtracked almost to where I got off I-495. In the morning I left Medway on SR109 to SR16 and then to SR140. US-2, which follows the Mohawk Trail, passes through N. Adams. Near a Shell gas station just west of town, I went south on Mt. Greylock Reservation Rd./Notch Rd. I did some extra driving to find it so here are some specifics: On Notch Rd, bear sharply to your left at 1.2 miles and right at 3.4 miles, for 8.5 miles to Summit Road on the left. Go .3 miles on Summit Rd to the large parking area (174).

#07

Mount Frissell, Connecticut
(2,380 feet)

Meeting Deer.

IT HARDLY SEEMS possible that I had traveled more than 1,600 miles before I saw my first and second deer on this trip, about 40 minutes before I arrived at the trailhead to Mt. Frissell.

As a professional truck driver, I have been taught to only apply brakes if I might hit a deer. Although I have been fortunate, I have seen that problems increase when truck drivers swerve to avoid deer. As a motorcyclist, I have learned that my options would be to brake and/or swerve, but not both at the same time. Since it is possible that swerving will put the deer back into the path of travel as the deer tries to move out of the way, I have resolved to only apply my brakes on a motorcycle if I might hit a deer. Fortunately, these two deer were along the roadway and not on it.

I was two and a half hours behind schedule when I parked our Wing and began the hike to Connecticut's highpoint. I knew it would soon be dark, so there was little time for stopping to smell the roses. I quickly changed into my hiking boots and started out on a dry path that was easy to follow. The trail would have been no problem even if I were wearing my riding boots.

From Mt. Washington Road near the state line, the path takes the hiker into Massachusetts then down into Connecticut via the summit of Round Mountain (2,296 feet). From there the trail crosses the state line again to reach the summit of Mt. Frissell in Massachusetts (2,453 feet) and then south again to the state line. At the highpoint is a stone cairn, which is on the Connecticut/Massachusetts state line (2,380 feet). The primary route is a moderate hike of 1.2 miles on a class l trail. East and slightly south of the state highpoint is Bear Mountain (2,316 feet) which is the highest mountaintop in Connecticut. Unlike most of the hikes, going up and coming back each took me an equal amount of time—about 45 minutes.

Ted Rybak, who lives in Waterbury, Connecticut, has maintained books of visitors who have signed in over the past 20 years. He hikes up a few times each year to check out the book that now fills up faster than during years gone by. He finds the thousands of entries in the several logs reflect fascinated visitors.

ROUTE:

From Mt. Greylock in MA: Mt. Greylock & Rockwell Rd. to US7 through Pittsfield to Great Barrington. SR23 to SR41 to Salisbury. At the junction of US-44 and SR41 proceed NW on Washinee Street for less than a mile. Turn left on Mt. Riga Road for 2.9 miles. Turn right (N) on Mt. Washington Road for 3.3 miles to the MA/CT state line. Park about 100 feet south of the state line (62).

08

High Point, New Jersey
(1,803 feet)

Am I that old?

T HE DAY I VISITED Mt. Frissell was the first time I made a mistake that could have cost me a lot of money for a place to sleep. It was 8:15 pm when I got back to our Wing, so by the time I got near a phone to make arrangements for a campsite, it was full. Not only was the KOA full, but its staff knew of no other campgrounds with vacancies. It was Friday night and evidently many had fled New York City to spend time with the beauty of nature.

I listened as a woman called around looking for a place to spend the night. After several calls, she called a family or friend and told of her problem of finding a place for the night. It sounded like everything was full, so when I heard the caller ask if they could just stop over and camp on their living room floor, I decided I would just kept driving. I had no friends or relatives in that area.

Why didn't I grab my *Gold Book* from my saddlebag? (It includes a list of the GWRRA members by city and state, including notes of those members who have lodging.) I didn't use that information because that takes something I don't have—courage to call unknown people even if they have offered lodging to other GWRRA members. Instead of calling someone from the *Gold Book*, I decided to just drive until something came up.

After an hour or so, I stopped at a motel with a vacancy sign out—the first vacancy I had seen that evening. No wonder they had vacancies. When the night clerk told me the price, I said I didn't want to make the mortgage payment, I just wanted a room for the night. He and one of the guests standing in the lobby agreed that the price was unreasonable.

The clerk said that all motels in that area were very expensive, but if I would go a little ways out of the area I should be able to find more reasonable prices. When he found out what way I was headed, he offered to call ahead to look for a room. I was very grateful for his help when he found a room at about a third of the cost. Riding extra miles that night put me well on my way to High Point, New Jersey, and ahead of schedule when I woke the next morning. My place of lodging for the night in Pleasant Valley, New York, was a bit out of route, but I was still ahead of schedule.

I had a leisurely big breakfast and was looking forward to this day about as much as any, but I took too much time eating. The crowd present for their first Saturday morning meal overwhelmed the staff, and that put me a little behind schedule once again.

My wife, Jeri, our youngest son Jason, three friends and I had already visited High Point, New Jersey during a motorcycle trip to Maine two years earlier, but this time I was to meet a nephew and his family. After many years of only seeing photos, the plan was to meet Mike and his family at High Point, then I would stay that night with another nephew.

High Point is located in the northwest corner of New Jersey. The 220-foot high monument at the summit is the highest structure on any state summit. It is just a short walk from the parking lot to the base of the monument, which may remind you of the Washington Monument in Washington, D. C., when you get your first glimpse of it.

The park was created with land donated by Colonel and Mrs. Anthony R. Kuser in 1923. The monument, completed in 1930, was also provided by the Kusers and is dedicated to New Jersey's wartime heroes.

As I approached the monument, I snapped a picture of what I thought were my nephew's two children standing at the top of the steps, between the flagpoles in front of the monument. What a picture! But it wasn't Ian and Mara. My nephew Mike, his wife Angie, and their son Ian were standing along the stone wall that surrounds the monument. They were enjoying the panoramic view of the countryside while Mara sat on the top of the wall. Although the top of the wall is wide, dad and daughter were in touch.

They had already climbed the stairs inside the monument and agreed that it was worth my time to go up. Since some of them agreed to go with me, I was obliged to take the 291 steps up. (I won't mention the one who found that the first time up and down was enough for her.) The steps go along the four walls of the monument, which leaves the middle open to look up and down its height. Along the way and at the summit are windows for viewing.

I have been surprised at how many lakes are found near highpoints, and New Jersey is no exception.

As we talked about years gone by, Mike made me feel old when he mentioned possible retirement from the Air Force in about three years. Could I be old enough to have a retired nephew? They were currently stationed at McGuire Air Force Base and made the trip just to meet me. They hadn't made reservations for camping yet, but had done some checking, so they knew their options. I had started thinking a lot about lodging plans because of my experience the night before.

We went down to the lake that we had seen from the summit. We laid on the beach, got wet, and had lunch on the blankets. We even saw a few fish swimming near the rope marking the limit of the swimming area. The beach facilities provide showers, a snack bar, and provided a refreshing environment in which to visit and play. We said our farewells after lunch, and I was on my way again. Most of my visits were too short, and that would have driven Jeri crazy!

ROUTE:

From Mt. Frissell in CT: Backtrack to US-44 past the NY state line then to Taconic State Pkwy to I84 to SR23 (Exit 1) to the visitor center on the left (147).

SIDE TRIP:

About 12 miles south on Beemerville Road (CR519) is Space Farms Zoo and Museum with 100 acres of wild animals, museums and attractions for the whole family.

#09

Ebright Azimuth, Delaware

(442 feet)

*Highpoints may appear to change
over the years—now 448 feet.*

I CROSSED FROM NEW Jersey into Pennsylvania on a stretch
of I-78 and almost immediately headed south on CR611. It was
already late afternoon, so when I saw a fresh fruit & vegetable
roadside stand, I stopped there to enjoy a few fruits and then
packed some vegetables to have for an evening snack. I would
not be arriving at my other nephew's home until late that
night.

Highpointer Jeff Stringer thinks Ebright Azimuth gets a
bad rap rather unfairly. In the Fourth Quarter 1996 *A to Z
Newsletter,* Jeff wrote that though Ebright Azimuth is one of
the lowest highpoints, it's actually one of the more unique
highpoints since it's in a residential neighborhood. Ironically,
he said it was one of the most difficult highpoints for him to
find, but admits that he didn't have one of the guidebooks.
When he finally got there, a delightful woman named Doreen,
who just happened to be out walking her dog, chatted with
him, had a book for him to sign, and told him about the area.

At a few of the highpoints, visitors question whether the

identified summit is the highest point in the state. Ebright Azimuth is often questioned since many think that the true highpoint may be in a lawn in the nearby trailer park, rather than the middle of the road. But Don W. Holmes, chairman of the board of the Highpointers Club, said a recent survey indicated the elevation under the sign was 448.25 feet and the benchmark near the entrance to the trailer park was 447.85 feet. The elevation near the eastern most mobile home in the trailer park is 450.85', but is obviously a man-made summit.

Having only casually observed the construction of roads, I would suspect that even the elevation under the sign might have been built up some by the road crew. This is one more example of why highpoint elevations and locations appear to be wrong and illustrates the importance of everyone acknowledging just one official elevation and location.

To see how elevations have changed over the years, consider the following comparison of 1996 accepted state highpoints compared to The *National Geographic* article of March 26, 1909, which identified the highest point in each state. These are listed in the order I visited them.

	1996	**1909**
NY	Mt. Marcy 5344 feet	same
VT	Mt. Mansfield 4393 feet	4406 feet
NH	Mt. Washington 6288 feet	6290 feet
ME	Mt. Katahdin 5267 feet	5268 feet
RI	Jerimoth Hill 812 feet	Durfee Hill 805 feet
MA	Mt. Greylock 3487 feet	3505 feet
CT	Mt. Frissell 2380 feet	Bear Mtn 2355 feet
NJ	High Point 1803 feet	1809 feet
DE	Ebright Azimuth 442 feet	2 summits 440+ feet
WV	Spruce Knob 4861 feet	4860 feet

1996	**1909**
MD Backbone Mtn 3360 feet	3400 feet
PA Mt. Davis 3213 feet	Blue Knob 3136 feet
OH Campbell Hill 1549 feet	1.5 mi E of Bellefontaine 1540 feet
IN Hoosier Hill 1257 feet	Randolph Co 1285 feet
KY Black Mtn 4139 feet	The Double, Harlan Co 4100 feet
VA Mt. Rogers 5729 feet	5719 feet
NC Mt. Mitchell 6684 feet	6711 feet
TN Clingmans Dome 6643 feet	Mt. Guyot 6636 feet
SC Sassafras Mtn 3560 feet	3548 feet
GA Brasstown Bald 4784 feet	4768 feet
AL Cheaha Mtn 2405 feet	Che-aw-ha Mtn. 2407 feet
FL Britton Hill 345 feet	Near Mt. Plesant Station 301 feet
MS Woodall Mtn 806 feet	Near Holly Springs 602 feet
MO Taum Sauk Mtn 1772 feet	Tom Sauk 1800 feet
AR Magazine Mtn 2753 feet	2800 feet
LA Driskill Mtn 535 feet	In western parishes 400+ feet
TX Guadalupe Peak 8749 feet	8690 feet
CO Mt. Elbert 14433 feet	14436 feet
KS Mt. Sunflower 4039 feet	W edge, N of AR River 4135 feet
OK Black Mesa 4973 feet	SW corner 4700+feet
NM Wheeler Peak 13161 feet	2 mi N of Truchas Peak 13306 feet
AZ Humphreys Peak 12633 feet	SanFrancisco Peak 12611 feet

46

1996	**1909**
CA Mt. Whitney 14494 feet	14501 feet
NV Boundary Peak 13140 feet	Wheeler Peak 13058 feet
OR Mt. Hood 11239 feet	11225 feet
WA Mt. Rainier 14410 feet	14363 feet
ID Borah Peak 12662 feet	Hyndman Peak 12078 feet
MT Granite Peak 12799 feet	12834 feet
WY Gannett Peak 13804 feet	Mt. Gannett 13785 feet
UT Kings Peak 13528 feet	Mt. Emmons 13428 feet
NE Panorama Pt 5424 feet	Plains in SW corner 5300+feet
SD Harney Peak 7242 feet	7240 feet
ND White Butte 3506 feet	S part Bowman County 3500+feet
IA High Point 1670 feet	5 mi SE of Sibley 1670 feet
IL Charles Mound 1235 feet	1257 feet
WI Timms Hill 1951 feet	Rib Hill 1940 feet
MN Eagle Mtn 2301 feet	Misquah Hills 2230 feet
MI Mt. Arvon 1979 feet	Porcupine Mtn 2023 feet

Don't be surprised to find different elevations—just check the date because highpoints appear to change over the years.

Delaware has no state sales tax and is recognized as the first state because it was the first to ratify the U.S. Constitution in 1787. It provides a comfortable climate with average temperatures in the summer of 76 degrees, and in the winter of 33 degrees. The first Europeans to settle in this area were Swedes under their captain, Peter Minuet, who arrived at the Wilmington waterfront in 1638. The Kalmar Nyckel Shipyard and Museum commemorates that first settlement.

ROUTE:

From High Point in NJ: SR23 to Colesville. SR519 through Uniontown to I-78. Cross the Delaware River to PA (65). Take SR611 (Exit 22) through Danboro. US-202 to DE then another mile to SR92. East (Left) to Ebright Rd and head north, less than a mile (166).

#10

Spruce Knob, West Virginia
(4,861 feet)

I'm no dentist!

AFTER EBRIGHT Azimuth, I continued to a nephew's home located west of Washington, D. C., for Saturday and Sunday nights. Ken had only recently moved with his wife, Tracy, and their boys, Joshua and Zachary, because his company asked him to relocate and take on a new project. When they lived near us in Michigan, we only occasionally saw them, but in two years of being in northern Virginia, I had already accepted their invitation to stay on three separate occasions.

As I had planned this trip, I intended to rest each Sunday so I arrived late Saturday evening, enjoyed worshipping with them and catching up on things on Sunday. All too soon it was Monday morning and time to put the sunrise in my mirrors. I had been warned to expect slow going as I got close to Spruce Knob in West Virginia and continued to Black Mountain and Mt. Davis, but my early start Monday put me well ahead of schedule. Some sources still show the elevation of Spruce Knob to be 4863 feet, but 4861 feet is the official elevation.

I left Ken and Tracy's in Centerville, Virginia, about 8:15 am on July 14th, entered West Virginia at 11:02 am and arrived at

Spruce Knob at 12:38 am, which was more than two hours earlier than I had planned. The weather that day was 75-85 degrees, so my long sleeve cotton shirt was comfortable even later in the day. It was hazy but not a cloud was in the sky. This was one of the areas where I would have liked to have spent a few days riding.

Spruce Knob is located in a 100,000-acre part of the Monongahela National Forest called Spruce Knob-Seneca Rocks National Recreation Area (NRA). Numerous activities in this area are managed in harmony. Timber harvests are designed to create openings beneficial for wildlife and create vistas as well as provide hardwood supplies. Cattle or sheep graze in many of the open areas, which helps keep them open as well as provide meat and wool. Some openings are leased for natural gas production. These openings built for gas wells are seeded with game-supporting grasses. Still other areas are leased to farmers who raise corn or hay, which adds to the rural agriculture landscape that has existed here for nearly 200 years. I was impressed. There was a true balance that is often lacking in other areas of our wonderful country.

I think most motorcyclists with a little experience have found they are able to take curves about 10 to 15 mph over the suggested limit. But those with more experience have found that things can alter those limits. It may be a logging truck going the other way, a squirrel crossing the road, gravel thrown onto the road by tires that have run onto the shoulder, etc. When you ride aggressively and close to the limit of you, your motorcycle, and the environment, you'll likely find yourself riding *beyond* those limits. Then you'll probably need some repair work on your bike and body. But it is fun to look through your turn and be able to see your antenna and rear speakers out of the corner of your eye!

Somewhere crossing the Allegheny Mountains I was practicing the cornering technique of "slow, look, lean, and roll" through numerous 15-35 mph switchbacks. There was almost no traffic to hear the occasional scraping of my foot pegs on the pavement. At one sharp right-hand double-back turn I found myself slowed to almost a dead stop. I didn't remember intentionally slowing so much, but am fortunate that I did. Shrubs, trees, and the mountain all blocked my vision around the turn, so I did not see the red logging truck heading in the opposite direction. He required both lanes plus the inside shoulder to get around the corner. Had I taken this turn at the speed I had taken the previous thirty-plus switchbacks I don't think I could have prevented hitting the truck or trailer.

When I shared that experience, I found that Charlotte Beach, from our church, had made a commitment to say a prayer for me each time she saw a motorcyclist while I was on this trip. Some call it luck. I call it traveling mercies and believe they have kept me from harm many times.

The last 9.2 miles to the summit were not paved, and much of the final route provided a 9 percent grade. With no rain in this area for several days, much of the road ended up covering the Wing and my face. Until this point in the trip, I used Mary Kay Sun Essentials, which is an oil-free sunblock. But with so much dust, I used a bandana to cover my face on my downhill trip.

I had several bandanas with me. When I encountered cold weather, I often used one to keep the draft away from my neck. But as the temperature rose, I used a wet bandana to reduce ring-around-the-collar and help keep me cool. When it got very hot, I often took the ice from my last drink and wrapped the chips in my bandana before securing it around my neck. Now one of my bandanas was serving another purpose as an air filter. I had seen other motorcyclists wearing bandanas to cover their faces but never tried it myself until now. It wasn't bad, so many days on the remainder of the trip I just used a second bandana to cover my face rather than use the sun-block.

The 9 percent grade is a steep incline. Translated into motorcycle terms, I was comfortable going up alone, and the Gold Wing has enough power to even take it in 5th gear.

Having a passenger would have been okay, but coming down was unnerving since I couldn't apply just my rear brake. When the rider of a Gold Wing presses the rear brake peddle, one of the two front brake sets is also applied, so the rider cannot apply the rear brake only. With limited traction on gravel roads, riders benefit by not using any traction for braking with the front wheel. It is better to leave all of the available traction for following the curves. Although the integrated braking system of the Gold Wing does a very good job in most situations, it does have some disadvantages. It could be very dangerous if one gets going too fast and needs to slow for a curve. I know that some of you riders suggest downshifting. That does help, but with such steep grades, downshifting doesn't always do a good job at slowing the bike down when you're already going too fast.

The ground hog I met along the road to the summit must have thought I was a dentist. He sat up tall and still and showed me his pearly white teeth! A doe and her fawn on the road near the top didn't seem to care if I was a dentist or not. They went bounding down the slope and into the brush, and left only a memory.

One-sided "flag" red spruces, deformed by constant exposure to strong westerly winds, are seen from all four sides of the stone and steel observation tower, which sits atop the Knob. The USGS benchmark is just north of the observation tower. A stroll along the half-mile *Whispering Spruce Trail*, which circles the Knob, will reveal blueberry and huckleberry bushes, which hug the ground. If you arrive a little later in the season than I did, you may find yourself snacking on the fruit they provide. Interpretive signs along the gentle, graveled trail describe the high country vegetation, geology and animal life. Be aware that snakes (timber rattlers and copperheads) may be found in the same rocky locations as the berry bushes, and remember that bears are fond of the berries, too. While harvesting berries for your own use is allowed, collecting plants or gathering their fruits to sell without a permit is illegal in the national forest.

Four cars were parked along Forest Service Road 112. I met one going down and saw two more at the top, so it is likely that you won't be alone when you visit the summit. It appeared that one of them with a small boat had already visited nearby Spruce Knob Lake, which provides the angler with a 25-acre impoundment regularly stocked with trout by the DNR. There are also brown and brook trout in the Gandy Creek and Seneca Creek drainages to the west of Spruce Knob. About 60 miles of established hiking trails are in the area with several more criss-crossing the woods and ridges.

Be prepared for cold fogs and strong winds even in summer months. On the way in, you may notice the Spruce Knob Picnic Area, which lies one-and-a-half miles south of the observation tower. You'll find that additional toilets, picnic tables and grills are nestled amongst a dense stand of spruce trees. If camping is your thing, you may try camping away from designated campgrounds as long as you pack out what you pack in and remove all traces of your visit.

Have fun, but use caution when riding. Whenever the roads appear to be drawn by a nervous or drunk mapmaker, I always expect a good ride. Roads in this area are narrow and winding and many have 40-mph speed limits.

ROUTE:

From Ebright Azimuth in DE: Ebright Rd to SR92 to SR100 to SR141 to SR2 through Newark to I-95. I-495 around Washington to I-66 to US15/29 to US211 to I-81 to Harrisonburg. US33 to WV then continue on US33 to SR28 and then west onto Forest Service Road 112 which is gravel for the last 9 miles (343).

#11

Backbone Mountain, Maryland

(3,360 feet)

Well marked, or too well marked?

AFTER LEAVING Spruce Knob, I stopped at another land-mark in that area. Seneca Rocks has long been noted as a scenic attraction and is popular with rock climbers, but it was purchased by the federal government in 1969. The rocks are a magnificent formation that rise nearly 900 feet above the North Fork River. The first European settlers in the region appeared around 1746. At that time, West Virginia (or Western Virginia, as it was then) was the edge of the great wilderness. Slowly the area was settled, disturbed by the events of the American Revolution and the Civil War, which pitted brother against brother in these border counties.

It is unknown who the first person was to climb Seneca Rocks. Undoubtedly Indians scaled the rocks prior to the European settlers that reached the area, but there is no record of their ascents. The historic ascent of Paul Brandt, Don Hubbard, and Sam Moore in 1939 found an inscription of "D.B. Sept. 16, 1908." This has been attributed to a surveyor named Bittenger who was known to be working in the area, according to Bill Webster in *Seneca, the Climber's Guide.*

The documented climbing history of the rocks began in 1935 with a roped ascent of the north peak by Paul Brandt and Florence Perry. In the 1930s and '40s, only a few climbers attempted to climb Seneca Rocks, but in 1943 and 44, the U. S. Army used the rocks to train mountain troops for action in the Apennines.

There are more than 375 major mapped climbing routes, varying in degree of difficulty. Only trained and experienced rock climbers should attempt to scale the rocks, however, a self-guided interpretive trail beginning behind the Seneca Rocks Visitor Center offers the non-climber a way to reach the lofty heights of the rocks and view the scenic valley below. The West Side Trail is 1.3 miles long and although steep, can be enjoyed by visitors of all ages. Steps, switchbacks and benches scattered along the trail all ease the ascent for visitors. At the top you'll be rewarded with a platform and lovely views of the valley below.

On my trip I noticed many interesting signs like the ones identifying Davis as the highest incorporated town in West Virginia. Colorado had two cities with similar claims and worked it out so that each can rightly claim to be the highest. I decided it was interesting enough to include in Chapter 28, since it illustrates one of the principles by which we should all live: "If it is possible, as much as depends on you, live peaceably with all men" (Romans 12:19 NIV).

The Western Maryland Railway owned the property, including Backbone Mountain, until CSX bought the railroad in 1980. Then Western Pocahontas Properties bought the property with other parcels from CSX Minerals of Richmond, Virginia, in 1987 for possible natural resources development. This is timber and coal country.

Although Backbone Mountain was envisioned in the 1974 Garrett County general plans as a possible site for a scenic highway (like Virginia's Skyline Drive), nothing came of it. No evidence suggests any push for a public park for this slight bump on the long ridge. Doug Toothman, manager of land resources for Western Pocahontas, said there are no plans to limit hiker access to Hoye-Crest area (named after Captain Charles Hoye, founder of the Garrett County Historical Society), but the company hopes hikers realize it is private land. Reverend John A. Grant (70+ years old) has led several trips to Maryland's highpoint and edits the *Glades Star* (quarterly news of Garrett County Historical Society).

Laurel was considered a name for this county, but local sentiment toward the Baltimore and Ohio Railroad was obvious when it overwhelmingly picked Garrett, in honor of John W. Garrett, who was president of the railroad in 1872.

If you are a history buff, you may find the creation of Garrett County interesting because it is unique in Maryland. A permissive clause for the creation of a county in the area, now included in the bounds of Garrett County, was inserted in the constitution of 1851 (Art 8, Sec 2). Nothing was done about the matter, however, until 1872, after two subsequent constitutions, 1864 and 1867, had provided that any new county must have an area of at least 400 square miles and a population of at least 10,000. Serious agitation for another western shore county began after the creation of Wicomico County on the eastern shore by the constitutional convention of 1867.

By 1871 it was conceded that all constitutional requirements had been met, and the assembly created Garrett County by act of April 1, 1872 (Acts 1872, ch 212). The bounds were fixed by the act:

> That all that part of Allegany County lying south and west of a line beginning at the summit of the Big Backbone, or Savage Mountain, where the mountain is crossed by Mason and Dixon's line, and running thence by a straight line to the middle of Savage River, where it empties into the Potomac River; thence by a straight line to the nearest point or boundary of the state of West Virginia; then with the said boundary to the Fairfax stone (headwaters of the Potomac), shall

be a new county, to be called the County of Garrett; provided the provisions of this act as to taking the census of the people and the area of said new county, and the sense of the people therein, shall be complied with in accordance with the constitution of this state.

The boundaries consist of straight lines on the west and north. Part of the line between West Virginia and Maryland is along the southeast bank of the Potomac River (whose waters are accordingly within the limits of Garrett County) on the southeast. The northern boundary, fixed by the part of the Mason and Dixon line which had no permanent markers, was not known exactly until the resurvey of that line was undertaken by the states of Maryland and Pennsylvania some time later.

The northeastern boundary was long in dispute because of the difficulty of surveying the line required by the act. The western line, which also marks the common boundary of Maryland and West Virginia, could not be drawn exactly until the boundary dispute between these two states was settled. When all its limits were fixed, Garrett County was found to have an area of 662 square miles, making it the second-largest county in the state. With about 40 persons per square mile, it's among the more sparsely populated counties in Maryland. If you are a scholar of Civil War battles, you may find it odd that none were fought in Garrett County.

Sugaring takes place in the late winter or early spring, as Garrett County continues to practice this art, which is older than the history of our nation. Indians tapped the trees long before the white man arrived, and though you may see tractors instead of horses, the production techniques are much the same. A maple tree must be about 40 years old before it is tapped.

The Maryland Department of Natural Resources has published some brochures indicating Backbone Mountain is in the Potomac State Forest with an elevation as only 3,220 feet. *The Garrett County and Deep Creek Lake 95-96 Vacation Guide* also mentions Backbone Mountain being in Potomac State

Forest with only an elevation of 2960 feet. Why the difference? It appears that the Backbone Mountain *Range* passes through the Potomac State Forest, but the highest point is located southwest of the forest with an elevation of 3360 feet. A historical marker was erected on the northern side of Route 50, just east of Redhouse, which may be about eight miles north of the actual highpoint. I parked off the pavement alongside a logging road more than four hours ahead of schedule. I evidently overcompensated for the cautions I received about not being able to make good time in this area. For those of us who enjoy an easy stroll through the woods, this can be one of our most pleasant experiences. Insects didn't bother me, and the trail was well marked with blazes — I hate getting lost! But you can't please everybody. I did read that at least one Highpointer complained that Maryland's highpoint area contaminated nature with too many blazes.

Within Garrett County, more than 70,000 acres of public land is available for hiking enthusiasts. Highpointers Gene & Lillian Elliot, who live in Silver Spring at the other end of the state, have placed certificates at the summit and have been working with Garrett County on improvements to the highpoint area. The Garret County Historical Society, in cooperation with the Boy Scouts, is maintaining the trail.

ROUTE:

From Spruce Knob in WV: Forest Service Road 112 back to US33 to Harman. SR32 to Thomas. US219 8 miles (1.7 miles south of SR24) to a logging road marked with a red sign on the right (E) side designating MD's highpoint (66). Park near the logging road entrance and proceed about 1 mile to the top noting trees marked in orange with either HP or an orange blaze. Bear left at the top and proceed about .3 miles to the top of boulders where WV/MD marker is located. Proceed down, then up small incline with trail turning left to Hoye-Crest highpoint sign. Hike is a little more than a mile and took me 27 minutes up and 25 minutes to get back down.

#12

Mount Davis, Pennsylvania
(3,213 feet)

Almost ignored by Pennsylvania.

The 67-mile ride from Backbone Mountain in Maryland to Mt. Davis went by all too quickly. Barry Ness, a fellow GWRRA member who lives in York at the other end of Pennsylvania, had recommended US219 as a good scenic riding road, and I wasn't disappointed with the quality, only the quantity.

When Barry and Denise first offered their help for my trip, they gave stuff I already had, but when they got my letter asking for more specific information, they fired back some great stuff from which you will also benefit. They had copied several pages out of two old books. At first I was disappointed because I wanted them to just summarize for me but was later very glad they did it their way. I benefited more from reading the uncut version than reading the summary/highlights I include in this chapter.

Pennsylvania is one of several states that appears to ignore its highpoint. Other than finding it on their official transportation map, I usually found versions of a typical one-liner like: "At 3213 feet, Mt. Davis is the highest point in Pennsylvania." If you're lucky, the one-liner might mention Summerset County but probably not that Mt. Davis is located on "the

Nigger." The 235-page 1996 *Visitors Guide*, for example, did not even list Mt. Davis or Negro Mountain in the index. I wasn't about to read everything in the guide to try to find something about the state highpoint.

Several variations of how Negro Mountain got its name exist, but in the 1906 publication of *History of Bedford and Somerset Counties Pennsylvania*, William H. Welfley wrote this version, which I chose to share.

> Captain Andrew Friend, one of the early pioneers who settled in the Turkeyfoot region, was a noted hunter and Indian fighter... On one of these excursions, which it is said was largely made for the purpose of exploring and viewing the country, occurred an incident which has given the Negro Mountain the name by which it is now known...

While fighting Indians, the Negro (most likely the Captain's slave) was wounded. The Negro believed he would die and urged Andrew Friend and another white man to leave him, but they did not. They hid in dense underbrush for the night, and the Negro died just before daylight.

> ...Friend and his companion had learned that blood of all brave men is of one color. From the earliest period of the settlement of those parts of Somerset county, this mountain has always been known and spoken of as the "Nigger" or Negro Mountain, and it has well been written that it is a great and grand monument to those three brave and heroic men of our earlier days, and that their story shall live while it endures.

Evidently it didn't endure because it's hard to find any current publications that indicate "Mt. Davis, in the northwestern part of Elk Lick Township on Negro Mountain, is the highest point in the state of Pennsylvania." That was recorded in The *Somerset County Outline* by John C. Cassady, who was a teacher in the schools of Somerset County (published 1932).

In 1753, at only 21 years of age, Lieutenant George Washington was in the company of Christopher Gist, who had been employed by the Ohio Company to find a route between Will's Creek and the Monongahela River land. They explored the area to include Negro Mountain. A few years later, after the French and Indian War (1754-59), troops under command of Colonel George Washington and General Braddock moved along Gist's route. In 1765, Governor Penn ordered that settlements in Indian lands be abandoned. Not only was that order ignored, westward migration increased. Settlers rushed west over the Cumberland Trail (US Route 40) and the very difficult Forbes Trail (US Route 30), but Negro Mountain remained mostly unoccupied. Early settlers on their way west found the Alleghenies difficult to cross.

Lumbermen cut the pine and hardwood forest from much of Negro Mountain between 1890 and 1930. Devastating fires also burned through the logging slash and consumed much of the organic matter. By 1929 the land was considered nearly worthless. The Commonwealth of Pennsylvania purchased the land from Ann Elmisa Humes for $3 per acre. Small parcels were also purchased from John N. Davis' heirs in 1931 and 1942. A Civilian Conservation Corps camp was established in June 1933 at a site on nearby Tub Mill Run and it made many improvements in four short years.

Mt. Davis was first given recognition as an area of special significance in 1945 when it was declared a state forest monument. A forest fire in the fall of 1951 resulted in a relative lack of mature vegetation in the highpoint area. Additional area around the highpoint was given protection by the Department of Forest and Waters so that it would remain in its natural state. In 1974, the Environmental Quality Board designated Mt. Davis as a natural area.

As I approached Mt. Davis, on a stretch of highway where US219 joins I-68, I again saw the familiar sight of three crosses on the north side, between mile markers 19 and 20. A pale blue cross stood to each side of an off-yellow one. No signs are present or necessary for travelers to be reminded of a very special payment that was made on our behalf almost 2,000 years ago.

Those sets of crosses were put up by Bernard Coffindaffer, a once-wealthy West Virginia businessman. He spent more than $2.5 million to put them up after a vision following open-heart surgery told him to start building *crosses of mercy*.

The first trio was built north of Charleston, West Virginia, and eventually some 1,800 were placed across 29 states. Coffindaffer painted these crosses, two pale-blue ones and a yellow one, to represent the colors of the sky and the light of the sun over Jerusalem. The crosses were also treated with a saline solution and built to last 35 years. Mr. Coffindaffer eventually went broke and died in October 1993, after more than ten years of building the *crosses of mercy*.

Along the stretch of US-219 & I-68 I was surprised to also see a small *Negro Mountain* sign along the shoulder. If I had not read the things Barry and Denise had sent, I would have probably missed the sign.

Mt. Davis is located midway between Meyersdale and Listonburg in southwestern Pennsylvania. It was named for John N. Davis, Civil War veteran, land surveyor, naturalist, and former owner of the site. An observation tower was constructed in 1935 by the Civilian Conservation Corps (CCC) and includes explanations of the rock formations on two plaques. An optical illusion leads one to believe that some of the surrounding area is higher. A large boulder a few yards west of the tower is the highpoint and has the USGS benchmark on it. Almost due north of the Mt. Davis observation tower (about 2 miles) is the Negro Mountain fire tower, which was constructed by CCC in 1934.

I approached Mt. Davis from the west, off of US-219 using County Road (CR) 669, which I do not recommend unless your bike is already dirty. When I left Mt. Davis, I was able to stay on paved roads, so I'll give those directions to the summit from US-40. It may be a little farther, but very pretty country throughout. I arrived at 6:20 pm on July 14th, just 35 minutes after crossing the state line, and I was almost 18 hours ahead of schedule, but for good reason. I was expecting to meet Howard Pletcher in Ohio.

The presence of Mennonite and Amish farms with their hardy lifestyle is obvious to even the casual traveler. You need not meet one of their black buggies along the roadway, but likely will.

ROUTE:

From Backbone Mountain in MD: US-219 to US-40 toward Uniontown. Near Addison watch for a large brown sign that points to "Youghiogheny Dam 8 miles." Head NE on SR523 a few miles and watch for SR2004 and "Mt. Davis 10 Miles." Follow the signs to the summit past a few views of lakes to the west. When you pass the YMCA Camp, you will be within 2 miles (67). This is recommended rather than going on US219, through Salisbury, to SR669 following the signs to Mt. Davis since that will involve gravel roads.

#13

Campbell Hill, Ohio
(1,549 feet)

Rushing to meet Howard.

I LEFT MT. DAVIS and started west on US-40 but was soon stopped by the lure of a roadside fruit & vegetable stand. It wasn't a balanced meal, but I surely did enjoy my supper of a few tomatoes, cucumbers, apricots, and a half-gallon of cherry cider (which I didn't finish until later, down the road). For the night I decided to stay at the KOA in Washington, Pennsylvania, where I had stayed a few times before. It is just 75 miles from Mt. Davis. When I arrived at 9 pm, I was well ahead of schedule, but it meant I didn't use SR21 and US-250 to pick up I-70, which is another very nice stretch I had been on before.

By noon the next day I was close to Campbell Hill and eight hours ahead of schedule, but I didn't stop. Instead, I headed for Indian Lake State Park campground, where I was to meet Howard Pletcher. Details for our meeting had not been finalized before I left Michigan, but we had both been in touch through Jeri during the past several days.

One of the requests I made before this trip was for people to contact Jeri if they were going to meet me along the way. She would always know if I was ahead, behind, or on schedule and then I would also know that someone was expecting me. This worked very well except in Wisconsin. I felt BAD about that one!

Howard was one of many who had responded to my plea for help in planning, executing, and writing a book about this adventure. From him I learned why so many of the round bales of hay were rotting in the fields. It seems there is a trend to move away from using the round bales because the farmers have found that their cows just weren't getting a square meal! He was also the first one with whom I had only corresponded and was going to meet for the first time. That was my reason for trying to get ahead of schedule since leaving Ken and Tracy's home near Washington, D. C.

The man I was to meet had been a reliability engineer and computer specialist with Navistar International (formerly International Harvester Truck Division) for nearly 30 years. He was interested in the history of most any form of transportation — trucks, tractors, railroads, canals, highways, etc., but had tried to find only one highpoint before we started corresponding. After looking for Ohio's highpoint on a map, he realized that he had been very close to it without knowing. I suspect he is not alone.

One thing Howard does is trace abandoned railroad rights-of-way across the countryside, so chasing highpoints couldn't be too strange for him. You might even catch him volunteering as a brakeman on the tourist railroad near the Hoosier High Point in Indiana. (See the next chapter about the Whitewater Valley Railroad).

Howard is a ham radio operator, photographer, and collector of toy tractors, trucks and International Harvester memorabilia. His part-time business involves finding parts for discontinued IH Scout 4WD vehicles, so I have little hope for him being free enough to fulfill his desire to travel some of Route 66 in the near future. Slow down Howard, you're making *me* tired.

The plan was for Howard to arrive first, from Fort Wayne, Indiana, and get a campsite, but I was too anxious to meet this guy with whom I had been corresponding for several months, so I got there first. That only messed up things a little. When he arrived, we picked a site, set up our tents, then went out to eat at a local mom & pop restaurant. Howard had been in the area before, so he took me on a little ride around the lake and pointed out some sights. Our campsite was next to another motorcyclist who had been at the campground several times before. I figured he knew where the best camping spots were.

In the morning Howard pulled out a portable CB and clipped it to the cover of the left pocket of our Wing's fairing. It would plug into my helmet's microphone and speakers system, and there was a Velcro strap with a push-to-talk button that he attached to my left handgrip.

As a trucker with a CB in my tractor, I'm not real fond of CBs most of the time. Too many....oh well, you know! But this was different. We each went to channel 7 as Howard escorted toward Campbell Hill. He had not been there before but was familiar with the area, and we had talked about our plans for the day. Later our plans did change, so they weren't set in concrete, but did include concrete.

We arrived at the summit at 8:50 am, took a few pictures, talked to a gentleman who was doing some work with a tractor, and left about 9:15 am. The Summit (some references show 1550 feet) is marked by a USGS benchmark that's embedded in concrete, flanked by a brick slab, and is 20 feet south of a flag pole on the property of Ohio Hi-Point Joint Vocational School, which is located two miles northeast of Bellefontaine. Permission to enter the property is not required, but the gate was only open from 7 am to 10 pm Monday through Thursday in the summer, and Monday through Friday when school was in session.

The Bellefontaine Air Force Station occupied this site and various buildings surrounding the highpoint before the school moved in. Many of the older military buildings and towers remain today.

ROUTE:

From Mt. Davis in PA: SR2004 to SR523 to US-40 to I-70 to Zanesville (Exit 153). SR146 through Nashport. SR16 and SR37 through Johnstown to Magnetic Springs. SR347 past East Liberty to US33 to Indian Lake State Park. Backtracking on US-33 the next morning to SR540 to Campbell Hill (300).

SIDE TRIPS:

In Bellefontaine, a monument marks the oldest Portland Cement concrete pavement in the U.S. Zane Caverns, about 5 miles east on SR 540, are noted for the rare cave pearl formations. On other trips, I had visited the Ohio Caverns, the AMA Museum located N of Columbus, and the USAF Museum in Dayton. We were within 25 miles of the Gold Wing plant in Marysville but didn't go see where our Gold Wing was built. Because of Howard's interest in the railroad, he took me to the Ex-DT&I Railroad bridge (98 feet high and 1,200 feet long) over the Miami River north of Quincy. Annie Oakley's birthplace is about 3 miles SW of Fort Loramie at a burg called Willowdale, and her grave site is about 1 mile south and 2 miles east of North Star. North of St. Mary's is Kossuth Deep Cut, a canal cut through a ridge that is about 100 feet deep and about a mile long and it still holds water. It becomes impressive when you look at it and learn that it was essentially hand dug!

#14

Hoosier High Point, Indiana
(1,257 feet)

Some call it Hoosier Hill.

A s HOWARD AND I departed Ohio's highpoint, we spent the morning seeing sights en route to Indiana. Our first stop was in downtown Bellefontaine, where we read about and examined the first concrete pavement in America, which was laid in 1891 around the courthouse building. Though it had been repaired, much of the initial concrete is still there, but no one was driving over it. Subsequent to this trip, I returned to find they have opened the area to traffic, so you may not always find things the same as you read in this book.

Other stops included the canal and railroad system summarized below. I would have missed it all without Howard's leadership and interest in the history-rich countryside. We missed the grave site and birthplace of Annie Oakley, which is near North Star, because I talked Howard into going through Troy, Ohio, instead. But he did take me for a walk along several preserved canal locks at Lockington.

By noon, I was growing attached to Howard's portable CB. Since we were going to pass close to Troy, Ohio, where Howard purchased his from Sierra Electronics, I convinced him to try to find the place. When we arrived in Troy, we searched a phone book and stopped by for my purchase. Howard donated his set of 9 AA batteries under one condition: He wanted to know how long the batteries last.

Previously unnamed, Indiana's highpoint was named by the Indiana legislature in June 1993. Hoosier High Point is in a grove of trees on private property owned by Kim Goble and Kathryn Knight of Richmond (as of Nov '89) and leased to Rob and Janet White who live there on Elliott Road. The highpoint is about 0.3 mile south of the intersection of Elliot and Randolph Roads at the south edge of a wooded area. You'll find a place to park just south of the woods on the west side of Elliot Rd. You may still see it referred to as Hoosier Hill, but that name is incorrect. A stile has been installed over the fence along the edge of the woods to permit easy access.

Mike Brewer of Terre Haute, Indiana, asked his represent-ative to have the state identify and name its highpoint. Along the way, the bill climbed a difficult hill. One editorial in the *Marion Chronicle* by Pete Beck was downright nasty and stated that naming the highest point in the state was a waste of time. But when the going got tough, Mike Brewer submitted a guest column concerning the editorial. The details can be found in the *Chronicle-Tribune* articles of early 1993, but suf-fice it to say Mike was persuasive enough to get it done. A pro-fessor at Taylor University, in a letter to Mike, complimented him on the rebuttal that was based on fact and had such a pos-itive tone. The professor closed his letter asking about the Highpointers Club.

A rough draft of a proposal was sent to Representative R. Jerome Kearns on October 27, 1992. Later two copies of the official edited and printed version of Preliminary Draft (PD) 3718 were also sent to Rep. Kearns. The PD was prepared by Legislative Services Agency 1993 General Assembly but did not include a name for the highpoint. Basically, the PD only required the Department of Transportation to erect signs and indicate its location on every state highway map prepared by the department. At the first regular session of the 108th General Assembly (1993), the proposed designation and name was enacted by House Bill No 1113.

It was read first on Jan 5, 1993, and referred to the Committee on Roads and Transportation. It was passed by the house in early 1993 as amended, then was sent to the senate. This bill was to amend the Indiana Code and can be found at www.law.indiana.edu/cgi-bin.

Be it enacted by the General Assembly at the State of Indiana Section 1. IC 8-23-23-4 is added to the Indiana Code as a new Section to read as follows:

Section 4.

(a) The point of highest elevation in Indiana is designated as 'Hoosier High Point.'

(b) The department shall erect and maintain signs to inform persons using the state highway system of the:

(1) location of; and

(2) way to the point of highest elevation in Indiana. The commissioner shall determine the design, the number, and the location of the signs required by this subsection.

(c) The location of the point of highest elevation in Indiana shall be indicated on each state highway map prepared by the department.

The map requirement required by IC 8-23-23-4(c), as added by this act applies only to state highway maps prepared after December 31, 1993.

As strange as it may first seem, the Hoosier High Point is not far from a valley with an interesting railroad history. Details regarding the history of the Whitewater Valley Railroad can be found in the Whitewater Valley Railroad's training manual, prepared by Professor Francis H. Parker of Ball State University, but here is a summary to whet your appetite.

Many of the early settlers prospered in Indiana, so there were surplus crops and mill products which needed to be transported to eastern markets, but transportation in the early 19th century was limited to roads that were muddy and slow at best, and not suited for heavy freight.

Water transportation was better suited for moving heavy freight. With the success of the Erie Canal, completed in 1825, there was a rush to build canals throughout the East and Midwest, where rivers were not navigable. Many public enterprises built and repaired connecting canals from 1824 to 1865 in an effort to provide a suitable method of moving the surplus crops and mill products to Eastern markets. That period was referred to as the Canal Era.

The Whitewater Canal was built on a difficult route with a fall of 491 feet in 76 miles. This required 56 locks, seven feeder dams and 12 aqueducts. The canal was built with an intended water surface width of 40 feet and a normal water depth of four feet. Along one side was a 10-foot wide towpath for horses.

Although the canal system promised to be a valuable transportation link, the Whitewater Valley Canal was never very successful. Four major floods plus constant smaller ones kept the canal unnavigable for long periods. When the canal didn't have too much water, it often had too little.

In 1864-65 the state legislature authorized a railroad along the canal route. The Canal Era ended in 1865 when the canal right-of-way was sold to the Indianapolis and Cincinnati Railroad.

The same internal improvements bill that had authorized the Whitewater Valley Canal in 1836 also authorized the Madison and Indianapolis as the first railroad in Indiana. Although this railroad began as a state railroad, it was transferred to a private company in 1843 before being given to Indianapolis in 1847. The Whitewater Valley Railroad was incorporated in 1865 and used the canal towpath as a convenient route for much of its length.

The Whitewater Valley Railroad struggled with many attempts to make it a meaningful part of the growing transportation system, but by the end of the 1800s, its life was all but over. There were other better and faster routes. Dwindling traffic led to all passenger service being dropped by 1933, but freight continued until October 1972. At that time, the light rails were not adequate for the modern freight cars.

The Whitewater Valley Railroad name was revived, with a slight change, in December 1972, when the current White Water Valley Railroad Company was incorporated as a not-for-profit corporation. It preserves and operates an historic railroad and displays steam railway equipment and conduct seminars. If you have time, stop in Connersville. Take a ride on the tourist railroad to Metamora, and you may even see Howard being a volunteer brakeman or conductor as you take a step back in time.

ROUTE:

From Campbell Hill in OH: SR540 to Bellefontaine. SR47 to SR235 to Quincy. (Take a peek at the Quincy Bridge) SR706 to Pasco. SR29 to Sidney. SR47 to Union City/State line. (Howard and I made a side trip down to Troy). Take SR227 south about 14 miles and turn west (right) on Randolph Road. In about a mile turn left on Elliot Road. About 0.3 of a mile at the edge of the woods is a pull-off area before a rolling field on the west side of Elliot Road between Randolph and Bethel Roads (100). The HP is a few yards back from the road and just inside the woods. In the summer of 1997 the commissioner had not yet determined that a sign should be posted along the road at this point.

#15

Black Mountain, Kentucky
(4,139 feet)

*Should it remain as private property or
become state owned?*

T HE ADDITIONAL TIME spent visiting and sightseeing with
Howard put me about six hours behind schedule. That's not a
complaint, just a fact that I needed to keep in mind as I
stopped at the KOA at Corbin, Kentucky, for the night (Exit 29
on I-75). It was about 100 miles from Black Mountain and left
a nice stretch of road for an early morning ride. The heat from
the day must have affected me more than I realized because I
slept until 6:30 am and was slow to be back on the road. I
wasn't underway until 8:30 am.

As one might expect from its name, much coal mining is
done in the Black Mountain area. In fact, the Kentucky Coal
Mining Museum is located in nearby Benham, Kentucky.
Some publications show Black Mountain's elevation to be
4,145 feet, which is higher than its acknowledged (official)
height.

As I approached the summit from SR160, I took the center
one of three paths about 150 yards past a large white FAA radar
dome. I was able to ride the center path to the tower and

antennas that were located at the peak. The old tower would probably offer a spectacular view of the area, but the lower steps had been removed to discourage climbers. Please respect the obvious desires of the owner and don't climb the tower.

Kentucky is one of several states with a privately owned highpoint and, as in the other states, some people want the state to pursue the purchase of the highpoint. At the time of my visit, several people were attempting to make improvements to Black Mountain, and even the landowner seemed amenable to some changes. Signs on the road that leads to the summit indicate that it is private property and there is no trespassing.

According to Highpointer Roger Rowlett, in his report shared in the Third Quarter 1999 *A to Z Newsletter*, the owner offered to sell the summit to the state of Kentucky for $10 million. I'm not convinced that it's any improvement to have states purchase their highpoints if the private owners will allow access to them. Roger Rowlett and Fred Lighty have worked with the owners to allow Highpointers to visit without the fear of being prosecuted for trespassing.

As of September 2, 1999, the Penn Virginia Coal Company has agreed to allow access to the summit for those who sign a waiver and send it back to them before their visit. A copy of that required waiver is included at the end of this book. If you attempt to access the summit without a prior waiver, you risk the possibility of being prosecuted for trespassing. When visiting, only the road to the highpoint may be traveled and, as always, respect other's property.

ROUTE:

From Hoosier Hill in IN: Elliot Road north to Randolph Road or south to Bethel Road. East to SR227 then south toward Richmond, US-27 to Liberty, SR101 (off of SR44) to Brookville. US-52 to I-74 to OH. I-74 to I-75 through Lexington to Exit 29. US-25E to US119 to Cumberland. SR160 to Black Mountain (358).

#16

Mount Rogers, Virginia
(5,729 feet)

Being behind schedule didn't help.

MT. ROGERS IS located in southwest Virginia within Jefferson National Forest on the Appalachian Trail close to North Carolina and Tennessee. The Appalachian Trail is the second longest footpath in the world and stretches over 2000 miles from Georgia to Maine.

There is more than one way to get to Mt. Rogers. I chose to hike from within the Grayson Highlands State Park. They charge $1 for daily parking. At the gate I received a map of the park, which included a legend with color-coding and mileage for the eight park trails. In addition, the map showed horse trails and the Appalachian Trail, which passes through the park and summit.

After being on the road for ten days and climbing to the summit of 13 of the first 15 highpoints, I must have considered myself an experienced hiker. I quickly made plans to start out on the Rhododendron Trail, marked with blue blazes. According to the map, the Rhododendron Trail would cross a horse trail and then cross the Appalachian Trail once before joining it. The Appalachian Trail would take me to the Mt.

Rogers summit. Easy enough, I thought. When I heard that the entire park stands above 5,000 feet, I didn't anticipate any difficult climbs or steep trails.

Do you tend to get extra frustrated or mad when you're a little pressed for time and things don't go as planned? Although I had made up a little time, I arrived at the Massie Gap parking area just less than five hours behind my schedule. Instead of arriving at 10 am, it was almost 3 pm so I quickly changed into my shorts and hiking boots. Anticipating an easy four mile hike up to the summit and another four back to the Wing, I figured I could make it up and back in a little over three hours, even though David Hauslohner of Troutdale, Virginia, suggested allowing five hours. Yep, I must have considered myself an experienced hiker. I would jog most of the way. I evidently am still learning that pride goeth before the fall, and the 5P rule: Prior Planning Prevents Poor Performance.

There were half a dozen vehicles in the parking lot. One group of four young people was preparing for a walk but knew nothing about Mt. Rogers. They all looked out of place—throwbacks from the '60s with hippie garb and hair, but young enough to have been born well after Woodstock. I admit to thinking they were probably off to the woodlands to do some drugs while bonding with nature.

I took off at a good pace, jogging along most of the Rhododendron Trail. I knew when I crossed the horse trail, but then I got lost within another mile. I doubled back and tried again, but knew I would have to move even faster to make it back to the Wing well before sunset. With my second attempt, I was still not confident that I was on the trail, so I decided Mt. Rogers would have to wait for another day. I did not want to end up lost because of my lack of preparation. Mt. Rogers was my first highpoint I had to record as a failed attempt. At Mt. Marcy, I arrived too late to attempt the summit hike and I had not planned to hike at Mt. Katahdin (because they don't allow motorcycles in the park). As I left Mt. Rogers, my highpoint record was now 13 of 16.

It would have been nice if Howard Pletcher (from Chapters 13 and 14) was still with me and I had a couple more days to spend here because the Virginia Creeper Trail sounded very interesting. It is located on the bed of an old abandoned railro a d right up Howard s alley.

The Creeper was built around the turn of the century to benefit from one of the last remaining stands of virgin forest in the east. From Abingdon, it runs approximately 37 miles up through an increasingly narrow gorge and along one of the most highly regarded native trout streams in Virginia. Trestles still carry the trail back and forth across streams with spectacular views of waterfalls and the gorge. There are several places where the trail can be accessed by vehicle to allow a short hike in either direction. The trail itself is easily manageable by anyone reasonably fit.

Grayson Highlands provides stables for guests who bring the types of horses that eat hay rather than sip gas. That area of the park provides 23 campsites that accommodate either tent or trailer with stalls for 67 horses. All horses must be sheltered in horse stable areas and are to be kept away from other camping, picnic, and visitor center areas. Although you may see them on the trail when you cross one of the horse trails, they should not take away from your enjoyment of the park. By calling their toll-free number, you can make reservations for a campsite or cabin: 1-800-933-PARK.

ROUTE:
From Black Mtn. in KY: SR160 to Appalachia. US BR23 through Norton. US ALT58 to Hansonville. US-19 through Abingdon. US-58 through Konnarock to Grayson Highlands State Park. Pick up the trail from the Massie Gap parking area (135).

#17

Mount Mitchell, North Carolina

(6,684 feet)

Tarantulas in North Carolina?

T HE 152 MILES between Mt. Rogers and Mt. Mitchell is beautiful mountain riding but took me four hours and 20 minutes. It was getting close to dark when I arrived at this drive-up highpoint located northeast of Asheville, several miles off the Blue Ridge Parkway. The road from the parkway gets closed at sundown, so I had very little time to spend at the summit — but what a beautiful sunset we had! Even the park ranger was a bit wrapped up in the sight. He said they seldom see the sun from Mt. Mitchell, so this was a real treat. I was reminded of an article Chuck Markham of Hico, Texas, had written in the December 1995 issue of *Wing World*. "...we are part of the lucky few who ever get to know this kind of elation and freedom. We have been to the top of the mountain on a steed that carries us as effortlessly as Pegasus, and returned, having seen things most mortals will never see."

This was my third time at Mt. Mitchell. My wife Jeri and our two boys had visited here when Jeremy and Jason were between five and ten years old. That time it was damp and cool, so the boys were wrapped in beach towels. I recall photographing a butterfly, which had landed along the path, and the fact that someone was buried at the summit stuck in my mind.

The second time I had been to the summit was with Brian Boers just two years earlier than this trip. That was during the same trip to Honda Hoot in Asheville when Jeri got me interested in highpoints — so it was the first one I intentionally sought out as a highpoint. The Honda Rider's Club of America hosts Honda Hoot. The second-annual Hoot was in 1995 and doubled as the AMA Southeast Regional Road Riding Convention for the year, so no matter what brand of motorcycle or type of riding preferred, all riders were welcome. Being in the Great Smokey Mountains National Park area provided a backdrop of motorcyclist's paradise.

The Blue Ridge Parkway is a 469-mile road, which provides wonderful motorcycle riding, but keep one eye on the road as you enjoy God's creation. In the summer of 1994 I found myself riding in the wet grass beside the parkway, which is not a suggested method of travel with a Gold Wing.

Mt. Mitchell was named in honor of Dr. Elisha Mitchell, a clergyman and University of North Carolina professor who explored the mountain. In 1835 he used a barometric measurement to determine the height of the mountain. He fell to his death on the mountain in 1857 at the age of 64 and is buried at the base of the observation tower.

This is not only the highest peak in the Eastern United States, but, as one would expect, acclaimed to be the coldest and windiest place in the Southeast.

Does North Carolina have tarantulas? Yes! One of the world's smallest tarantulas, the spruce-fir moss spider (*Microhexura montiuaga*) lives here. While most tarantulas are large and hairy, the diminutive spruce-fir moss spider is only two millimeters long. It would take 10 of these spiders, arm-in-arm, to reach across a penny. As the name suggests, they live in high elevation spruce-fir forests among moss-covered boulders. First discovered on Mt. Mitchell in 1928, surveys in recent years have only yielded two other populations, so not only are they small in size, but also in number.

ROUTE:

From Mt. Rogers in VA: US58 to Mouth of Wilson. SR16 to Glendale Springs. Blue Ridge Pkwy to the cutoff for Mt. Mitchell (152).

#18

Clingmans Dome, Tennessee
(6,643 feet)

Kamping Kabins

REMEMBERING THE difficulty I had with lodging en route to High Point, New Jersey, about a week earlier, and realizing I would be riding until late, I decided to call ahead to reserve a campsite. My destination was the KOA at Cherokee, North Carolina, and I was still behind schedule. From the KOA directory I expected a large campground, called the toll-free number, and reserved a tent space.

On previous motorcycle trips with my wife Jeri, we often enjoyed utilizing the KOA Kamping Kabins. Since the KOA in Cherokee has 106 cabins, I thought I would introduce this method of camping to those of you who haven't tried it. Kabins are not for everybody, but have their advantages.

We often travel with our youngest son Jason, and Brian, his friend from high school who has become a friend of the whole family. Even on occasions when we have the pleasure of another bike or two, the Kamping Kabins are still beneficial. KOA Kabins have either one or two rooms with the same basic design throughout the country. The one-room Kabin has a double bed and a pair of bunk beds, which is just right for four.

The two-room Kabin has the double bed in a back room and two pair of bunk beds in the front room to sleep six. They both have a porch.

We have found some minor differences with amenities, but you will likely find a small table inside and either a bench or swing on the front porch. In hot climates, we have had Kabins with air conditioners — now that's ruffin' it in comfort. Many have ceiling fans, and in the cooler places a heater is included or, as with the Cherokee KOA, electric heaters are available for rent. Water spigots are usually nearby, and for the TV junkies, cable hook-up is even available with the Kamping Kabins at the Cherokee KOA.

Advantages of the Kamping Kabins that we have found include the fact that we can all be together for those *UNO* games after supper and showers. If it rains or there is heavy dew, everything inside the cabin is dry, and when we pack up in the morning we don't have to put away a damp tent. Of course Jeri would say the biggest benefit is not having to sleep on the ground, and I'm glad I don't have to add a tent and cot to my list of things to pack.

On the flip side is the list of disadvantages. Jeri and I made two, three-week trips in the summer of 1996 using the KOA Kamping Kabins whenever we could. We found that most KOAs that have Kabins only have a few, so reservations are very important. Where the KOAs were located played a big part of our plans, but that in itself was usually not a problem. During our trip to California that year, we had one difficult day with strong winds from the south while we were headed west. When we stopped for fuel in the early afternoon, Jeri got off the bike at Little America and said she was not going any farther! We were both very tired of being beaten by the wind, but we had reservations just about 30 miles up the road. I knew a motel at Little America would be costly, and we would still be charged for the Kabin since most have a 24-hour cancellation provision.

We enjoyed a nice meal, did some window shopping in the

stores, and then I bought her an ice cream cone. It worked! We did get back on the road (a few hours after we stopped) and the wind did seem to die down as the sun was setting. We made it to our Kabin, but the fact that we were committed to a specific distance each day was a disadvantage to us.

The fact that restrooms and showers are not self-contained in the Kabins is not a disadvantage to us yet. We usually make it through the night without having to get up, but when morning breaks, we get dressed before going to the restroom. By the time we return, we're wide-awake and usually start packing. Kabins cost more than a tent space, but usually less than a motel. During this six-week trip, I started thinking seriously about the advantages of a camper behind the bike. Almost no reservations would ever be required, and the freedom of traveling more or less than our average would be worth something.

I arrived at the KOA in Cherokee, North Carolina, just before their *Absolute Quiet-Time* of 11 pm and set my tent up with just the light provided by the bathhouse and laundry across the way. After a week and a half on the road, everything had settled into just one place to be packed, so I needed very little light to pitch the tent, shower and settle down for the night. Before leaving the subject of staying at this KOA, allow me to mention the all you can eat breakfast of either pancakes or biscuits & gravy for $2.29. Add sausage or bacon, and orange juice, coffee or milk and it's only $3.79. I had breakfast there so I wouldn't have to stop again before I got to Clingmans Dome.

According to my odometer, the distance from Mt. Mitchell to Clingmans Dome was 123 miles. Visibility on the day I visited this and the next two highpoints was not good, but I'll wait until telling about Basstown Bald to explain why.

Originally known as Smoky Dome, Clingmans Dome was renamed for Thomas Lanier Clingman, U.S. senator, mining prospector, and Civil War general who explored these mountains during the 1850s. Accidents happen and sometimes set history. Thomas Lanier Clingman was a thorough North Carolinian, but his name is attached to the Tennessee highpoint. Born in Huntersville, North Carolina, on July 27, 1812, he graduated from the University of North Carolina (UNC) in 1832. On the faculty was a professor named Elisha Mitchell (after whom Mt. Mitchell is named). Both Clingman and Mitchell spent time in the Appalachians. Both claimed to have measured the highest peak in North Carolina. Although Mitchell was a Connecticut Yankee who went south in 1817 to teach at UNC, when Mitchell fell to his death near the summit in North Carolina, naming the mountain as a memorial tribute became a foregone conclusion.

It was Arnold Henry Guyot who named Clingmans Dome, and there was another whole feud over calling it Buckley Peak or Clingmans Dome. You see who won that! Clingman lost one in North Carolina, but won one in nearby Tennessee.

Clingmans Dome is located on the Appalachian Trail along the Tennessee/North Carolina border, almost in the middle of the Great Smoky Mountains National Park and may be the most visited of all the state highpoints. There is no fee to enter the Great Smoky Mountains National Park. This is not true of many other national parks.

A hike to the summit's lookout tower near the USGS benchmark is only a half-mile easy walk on a paved trail once you find the Forney Ridge parking area. The tower even has a ramp to the top for the handicapped.

Highpointer Kevin Williamson was the first one I knew to raise the question of whether Clingmans Dome is the highpoint of Tennessee. He had talked with a park ranger and a state employee who said a new survey was done with a laser and Clingmans Dome is lower than the summit of Mt. LaConte. Since that initial revelation, Kevin has had no information to verify what would normally be reliable information. This is just one more illustration of why the Highpointers Club waits for the USGS to consider elevations as official.

ROUTE:

From Mt. Mitchell in NC: Blue Ridge Pkwy to I-40 to US-19 to US-441 to TN (123).

SIDE TRIPS:

Cherokee, North Carolina, has much to offer. On the top of my list is the outdoor drama *Unto These Hills,* which tells the tragic yet triumphant story of the Cherokee Indians from early times to the present. The play was in its 47th season and often sells out, so reservations are almost a necessity. It's one of America's most popular outdoor dramas, set against the backdrop of the Smoky Mountains. Cherokee KOA holds a block of reserved seats — claimed to be the best seats in the house. Parking can be a problem since some of the parking lots are 1,200 yards down the hill, but the KOA buses get premium parking slots right by the entrance.

#19

Sassafras Mountain, South Carolina
(3,560 feet)

The Great Blue Hills of God.

Iₙ 1998, THE Highpointers 12th Annual Konvention was held in South Carolina and hosted by Highpointers Bruce and Sharon Nelker.

Sassafras Mountain is located in northwest South Carolina in a region called *Upcountry,* where the average winter and summer temperatures are low 40s and high 70s. It is not surprising to find conflicting information on highpoint elevations, but unlike other states that advertise higher elevations than recognized by the USGS, the 1996 Spring/Summer issue of *South Carolina's Upcountry* recorded an elevation of only 3,554 feet.

In 1776, Richard Paris, owner of a trading post in what is now downtown Greenville, married a Cherokee woman. His trading post was instrumental in bringing the first official white settlement in the South Carolina hills. Treaties with the Native Americans opened up what was called the Pendleton District — now Anderson, Pickens and Oconee Counties —

and in the 1780s the land-hungry flowed in. The next decade brought the South the cotton gin.

As Ben Robertson wrote in *Red Hills and Cotton* "Our wagon was hitched to cotton's star...Cotton is a state of mind with us, a philosophy, and we continue to plant it in spite of the fact that we have not made money on cotton more than once in about every ten years." That might be said of most farming, but cotton was their gift and curse; it had its particular effect.

As cotton wore out the land, it brought in the textile mills. While textiles remain the major industrial base, a diverse and growing range of manufacturing and business has also found its way here from all over the world. Tires from France, pumps from Finland, motor parts from Japan and cars from Germany are only a few of the industries that have since put down roots in these red hills. Its big crop is no longer cotton, but peaches. You'll also find quite a large crop of apples.

When you arrive at the parking lot, you'll be only about 100 yards from the summit marker, but as with a few other highpoints, you'll have no view of the countryside.

The Cherokee Indians who lived in Upcountry until the early 1800s called these beautiful foothills *The Great Blue Hills of God*, and evidence of their life in the area still abounds.

ROUTE:

From Clingmans Dome in TN: US-441 to Blue Ridge Pkwy to SR215 to Rosman. US-178 to CR199. Right 4.8 miles to a locked gate (113). You'll be going past Rocky Bottom Camp of the Blind. From the map, you'll see that you are very close to the NC/SC state line.

SIDE TRIPS:

How about some white water rafting? Starting high in the Carolina mountains and dropping an average of 49.3 feet per mile for 40 miles, the Chattooga River separates South

Carolina from Georgia. Once familiar only to local folk, the Chattooga, designated the South's first National Wild and Scenic River in 1974, became a sort of national quest after its starring role in the movie *Deliverance*. Rafting, canoeing and kayaking the Chattooga are now major adventures in the Upcountry.

Located at the Keowee-Toxaway State Park near Sunset is the Cherokee Indian Interpretive Center. This museum traces the history and culture of the Cherokee Indians who once lived in the Keowee Valley. Although it has free admission, it is not always open during the day.

If you enjoy old things that still work, try the Hagood Mill in Pickens. The restored 1825-grist mill is the only mill in South Carolina that uses the original wheel components. It is open all year during the day and charges no admission.

More than 50 waterfalls are in the region. The Issaqueena Falls, located in Stumphouse Tunnel Park, drop about 200 feet and is one of the most visited waterfalls in the Upcountry. Legend has it that an Indian maiden, Issaqueena, pretended to leap to her death in an attempt to escape hostile pursuers, but actually took refuge on a ledge beneath the falls.

#20

Brasstown Bald, Georgia
(4,784 feet)

New Green Place became Brasstown Bald?

AFTER LEAVING SASSAFRAS Mountain, while on US-76, I crossed the Appalachian Trail again. My route had me criss-cross the Appalachian Trail several times since I left Vermont's highpoint. Within about 20 miles after leaving Georgia's high-point, I would cross the Appalachian Trail for one last time. The southern end of the Appalachian Trail and Georgia's high-point and are both located in the Chattahoochee National Forest in northeast Georgia.

Since I arrived late in the day, the guard was gone and their honor system was in place. Parking at Brasstown Bald was $1, so I followed the directions by placing my dollar in an enve-lope, removing a tab to be placed on our Wing, and dropping the envelope into their box. The visitor center has exhibits, a video program, and a 360-degree observation deck with a panoramic view of four states. The United States Forestry Service provides a museum with free admission. You will also find picnicking and hiking areas and a craft shop. I arrived too late on Friday to enter the tower or theater.

It was while I was listening to a local radio station that I understood the poor visibility I had experienced that day visiting three highpoints. Reports were made of record-high pollution in the air. That record high must have been relatively low when compared with other places because I didn't notice my eyes burning, as I had experienced first in San Diego, California, when I was there for Boot Camp in 1966.

Near the parking lot is a concession stand with a memorial to Judge T. S. Candler of the Georgia Supreme Court, which was placed there in recognition of his dedicated service to the citizens of Georgia and the nation. His cooperative efforts made possible the construction of the Forest Service Visitors Center there. The plaque was dedicated in June 1971.

With such an unusual name as Brasstown Bald, I expected to find an interesting story about how it received its name, but the story is a little confusing. Brasstown Bald is derived from the Cherokee word *Itse'yi* (New Green Place) or (Place of Fresh Green), from *Itse'hi* (green or unripe vegetation) and yi the locative. It occurs in several places in the old Cherokee country, variously spelled *Echia, Echoee, Etchowee,* and sometimes Brasstown, from a confusion of *Itse'yi* with *Untsaiyl'* (brass). One settlement known to the whites as Brasstown was on upper Brasstown Creek of Hiwassee River directly northwest of the summit. I'm still confused—are you?

Every highpoint can have something very special about it, and Brasstown Bald is no exception. It was here that Michael Stewart visited his first highpoint in 1982. The second quarter 1997 of the *Apex to Zenith Newsletter* gave Michael's account of how he got started as a Highpointer with Brasstown Bald.

> ...while rock climbing in north Georgia, a buddy from McKinley asked if we could go to Brasstown Bald before heading home. Asking why, Eric informed me of his goal to reach the highest point in each of the United States. At the time, I found the idea of a real 'climber' driving up a bunch of hills as patiently absurd and told him so. A good-natured debate

ensued and we finally drove up Brasstown Bald with me constantly needling Eric about needing oxygen, belays, ropes, etc. To cap this off, returning from a climbing summer in Europe the following year, I drove from NY to Atlanta and hit every highpoint on the way to go one up on Eric (sending a post card from each stop). He drove to Missouri from his hometown in Tennessee the next weekend to tie us up. So I hit Alabama a week later to keep the rub going. Well, somewhere along the way, I got hooked. Sure, this wasn't world class mountaineering, but it certainly held its own brand of challenge and novelty. It was not unlike collecting rare and unique baseball cards, except that it required a...lot more effort.

Just as Michael got hooked on highpointing because of a friend, this strange urge was passed on to his son Josh at 9 years old to make it to the summits of the states. At 13, Josh Stewart became the world's youngest to climb all fifty state highpoints on December 22, 1996. Regardless of how soon someone younger breaks his record, Josh deserves a standing ovation, and it all started at this drive-up highpoint.

ROUTE:

From Sassafras Mountain in SC: US-178 to Rosman, NC. US64 to Highlands. SR106 through Scaly Mtn. US-23/441 to Clayton, GA. US-76 to Hiawassee. SR17 to SR180 to Brasstown Bald (120). (With more time to see the sights, I probably would have gone south from Sassafras Mountain on US-178 to SR11 which is also called the Cherokee Foothills Scenic Highway.)

SIDE TRIPS:

About 30 miles south on US-19 is Dahlonega, a Cherokee word meaning precious yellow metal, which is the site of America's first major gold rush in 1828. If you have time, you may try your hand panning at Crisson's Gold Mine and discover for yourself the phrase coined in that area: "thar's gold in them thar hills." The old courthouse in the center of the town square is now the Gold Museum with a film and exhibits which tell the story of the nation's first gold rush and describes mining techniques and the lifestyles of the miners of that time. The tour of Consolidated Gold Mines, once the largest mining operation in the East, takes visitors 250 feet into the tunnel systems made by miners more than a hundred years ago.

#21

Cheaha Mountain, Alabama
(2,405 feet)

Learn about the CCC.

US-19 FROM BRASSTOWN Bald was a wonderful ride on new, wide blacktop. The last stretch before Cheaha Mountain on Talladega Scenic Drive was also a beautiful road, comparable to the Blue Ridge Parkway.

Some say Cheaha (an Indian word for high) Mountain is 2407 feet. In fact, everything I saw in the area indicated this higher elevation. I arrived at the gift shop and entrance to the park at 11:15 am and was at the summit 25 minutes later. The weather was very nice, which was normal, but my next highpoint was experiencing a hurricane! How long could I continue enjoying a light wind, little white clouds, and the perfect temperature of 75 degrees? Near the entrance is a gazebo with a swing in it. I knew Jeri would enjoy that. Just beyond the gazebo, on the left, was a motel to provide accommodations to those wanting to stay overnight, but not wanting to camp.

Cheaha State Park is an old-fashioned 2,719-acre piece of land that doesn't give you the feeling that Holiday Inn arrived ahead of you. On a hot day you may want to go for a swim in the lake at the base of the mountain and use the bathhouse developed by the Civilian Conservation Corps (CCC) in the 1930s. The park includes the CCC Museum that was only open weekends from 11:30 am to 3 pm.

You may want to try the half-mile Bald Rock Trail or the Pulpit Rock Trail. Just follow the signs. For the more adventuresome, there is a ten-mile Odum Scout Trail which is part of the Pinhoti Trail System that passes through the park. Approximately 80 miles of the Pinhoti Trail System was completed, but your choices don't end there. The hardy might enjoy the steep mile-long Lake Trail.

Since Cheaha is so far from state lines, you'll see only one state but will feel like you see a lot of Alabama if you visit on a clear day. It was acquired by the state, along with 10 other state parks, between 1927 and 1933, but its official opening date was not until June 7, 1939. Many of the developments installed under the CCC remain and form the nucleus of the present day park system.

ROUTE:

From Brasstown Bald in GA: SR180 to US-19 to I-285 around Atlanta to I-20 to AL. I-20 to US-431 (Exit 191) to SR281 (Talladega Scenic Drive) to Cheaha Mountain (197).

#22

Britton Hill, Florida
(345 feet)

Kept away by Danny.

As I approached Cheaha Mountain from Atlanta, Georgia, on I-20, I stopped at the Alabama Information Center to call Rand Wortman about my plans for Britton Hill. Rand lives in Panama City, Florida, and is one of those who replied to my plea for help in planning, executing and writing this book.

Late July is early hurricane season. Weather and news on the radio had been telling about Hurricane Danny heading for the panhandle of Florida, which is the location of Britton Hill. Being from Michigan and having limited experience with hurricanes, their reports of tropical depression and feeder bans didn't help me much. I knew what their forecast for 20 inches of rain would mean, and I didn't mind the idea of getting the bike wet. The forecast included reports of 30-70 mph winds — been there, done that — but called Rand anyway.

When he answered the phone, his comment was something like "'Guess you're kinda wet; where are you?" I was far enough away to be enjoying nice weather, and he suggested it might be wisest to not run into Florida. I wanted to make it into all the states, but I have learned that it is often wise to listen to the recommendation of others. If I don't have a rec-ommendation, I try to learn by the mistakes of others before I am willing to learn by my own mistake.

Several years ago, a young girl was attempting some lengthy flight with her flight instructor. As she was attempting to leave one high-elevation airport (where the air was thinner) in weather that was not the best, she crashed.

My oldest brother Stan taught aviation and had read the particulars on that accident investigation. Stan has also helped students set records and accomplish goals, but was very wise about not letting a plan or schedule force him to do something unsafe. Had there not been people waiting at her next destination, maybe that young girl and instructor would not have decided to press on until after the weather improved. They might be alive today.

I was looking forward to meeting Rand for the first time, but I followed his recommendation to not head into Hurricane Danny. As it turned out, Danny stayed over Mobile, Alabama, quite a while before moving on. Sunday's report had accounts of 20-27 inches of rain in the Florida panhandle — but I stayed safe and dry up north.

The quest for any highpoint can be special and cause us to do some things out of the ordinary. Doug Heroux and Kathy Bishop, from South Windsor, Connecticut, arrived at the Pensacola airport and took a limousine to visit Britton Hill. The driver was initially overwhelmed by the fact that people would come from far and wide to this little picnic area but he now claims to be an expert on Florida's highpoint.

#23

Woodall Mountain, Mississippi
(806 feet)

Almost two days ahead of schedule.

FOUR BANK SIGNS in Annison, just north of Cheaha Mountain, showed the temperature was 96, 94, 95 and 97 while the thermometer on our GW showed 90-91 degrees. I started thinking that my thermometer was not accurate. When I installed it, I tried to calibrate it at 70 degrees. It appeared to be less accurate as it got farther from 70 degrees, but later that evening I passed another bank sign, which said it was down to 89 degrees, which was what my thermometer showed. What does that all mean? Nothing, except maybe bank signs are about as accurate as my $2.95 thermometer.

Because Hurricane Danny was to the south along the coast and caused me to skip Florida's highpoint, I arrived at Woodall Mountain almost two full days ahead of schedule.

With just over 800 feet of elevation, one might expect this highpoint to be on very level land, and it is. However, this is literally a mountain that drops about 200 feet of elevation steeply on all sides, so from a distance it is easily identifiable.

Fellow Highpointer Jack Graybill reported that about a

year earlier, at the entrance to the road up the mountain, there was an aluminum gate, but it was open. Tied to the gate was a decidedly unfriendly sign that read: "No unauthorized personnel beyond this point." The summit was trashed but the benchmark was not hard to find—almost in the exact center of the summit. When I arrived, I saw no sign and the summit was relatively well policed. There has been some talk of paving the mile of gravel road that leads to the summit.

ROUTE:

From Britton Hill in FL: If I had made it to Britton Hill, I was planning to head north on US-331 to Montgomery, then take US-82 to Tuscaloosa. US-43 to Hamilton. Since I skipped Florida, I arrived at Hamilton from Birmingham on US-78 then US-43. SR4 to SR19 to Belmont, MS. Take SR25 almost to US-72. CR187 is a loop off of SR25. CR187 joins SR25 about 2 miles south of US-72 and again 1/10 mile south of US72 and is along the west side. From about the middle of CR187, take CR176 for 7/10 mile. The one-mile gravel road to the summit will be to your right.

#24

Taum Sauk Mountain, Missouri
(1,772 feet)

Indian Language Trees.

SATURDAY EVENING I dodged a few thunderstorms with some heavy winds until I stopped late that evening. I called my new friend, Jack Longacre, who lives near Taum Sauk, but his answering machine took my message. Jack is the president of the Highpointers Club and the one whose small notice in *Outside Magazine* brought a handful of people together who encouraged him to start a club.

After a good night of rest, I had planed to do laundry and change my engine oil. I also decided to visit Taum Sauk on Sunday — my only Sunday travel on this trip. I did my wash, and while my clothes were in the dryer I found a garage where I rented a bay to change the oil. It was worth a few bucks to have them take my old oil. Back to the laundry mat to fold clothes, then I returned to my room where I left most of my things. Before I headed up to Taum Sauk about 11:15 am, I left another message on Jack's machine.

About 20 minutes up I-55 I realized that I didn't make note of where the motel was. Since I had skipped Britton Hill in

Florida, I was ahead of schedule. I spent Saturday night and was planning to spend Sunday night at the same motel somewhere in southeast Missouri along I-55. I did some quick computing based on what my mileage was then, and what yard stick (mile marker) I was passing. Then I had a fair idea where I should find my motel. I very much appreciate states that use the mile markers to also indicate the exit #, unlike Pennsylvania, Florida and a few others that just number exits sequentially.

On the way into the park, I stopped at Jack's, but there was no sign of him. I left a message in his message box—yes, he gets so many visitors stopping by that he has a box for notes—not just a mailbox. It was nice to have a lighter load since his driveway has a lot of large loose gravel. Another motorcyclist who had stopped by to see Jack on another trip told me he went down in Jack's driveway with his BMW. These big bikes can be difficult to handle off-road.

Jim P. (I won't use his last name) wrote about his experience at the summit and the view from the 100-foot fire tower. Although the tower does provide a nice view and it was the first place I went to when I arrived in the area, the first time I was there, I was a bit surprised that I didn't see a sign saying it was the highest point in the state. That's because it is not at the highpoint — sorry Jim, wrong spot!

Previously owned by James and Dorothy Roe, the land surrounding the highpoint was purchased in July 1991 by the Missouri State Parks system. Instead of taking the fork to the left where the tower is located, continue on the gravel road to a large parking lot.

Along the edge of the parking lot are information boards and the beginning of a relatively new cement path. Follow the path about 1,100 feet. There is a sign about eight feet up on a tree near the large rock at the summit.

Although the best view is from the lookout tower, the area is deceptively flat. For years Mr. Roe and the forest rangers at the tower have mistakenly directed seekers of the highpoint to the wrong spot, about 7.5 feet lower than the highest point. The highest point was found and documented by USGS surveyor Fred Lenz in 1957, but was neither marked nor monumented at that time. In 1968 the USGS completed topographic maps using aerial photographs to establish the highpoint as being 13 feet higher than the base of the lookout tower. Still, the highpoint had not been marked, so in April 1988, Highpointers Paul L. Zumwalt and his wife Lila, using a plane table and alidade, verified the location shown on the map he carried.

Having seen Daniel Boone-type movies at a younger age, I had picked up the idea that Indians had used trees to mark as well as read trails, but it wasn't until April 1997, when I visited Jack Longacre, that I learned a little about thong trees, sometimes called Indian Language Trees. Most thong trees are white oaks which were bent to a horizontal position when saplings and held that way by forked sticks called thongs. One or more of the branches were allowed to grow vertically from the horizontal section. Indians would often add meaning to the deformed tree by blazes or carvings on the knee or nose, which are the outsides of the bend. In recent years the Arcadia Valley Garden Club in nearby Ironton, Missouri, has been working to expand public appreciation of these living Indian relics. Contact Rita Hadley, Rt. 1 Box 97A-1, Annapolis, MO 63620.

Most known thong trees are about 55 inches in circumference and were bent about 150 years ago. If you suspect a tree is a thong tree, you are asked to photograph it, record the location, note the species of tree, and measure the circumference halfway between the ground and first bend. The local archaeological society will want to verify it since Mother Nature can bend a tree. These casualties by Mother Nature will differ from true thong trees, which are usually scarred by the thongs at the bends.

Jack Longacre, who lives along Highway CC (3.1 miles) leading up to the highpoint, has located at least a dozen thong trees while out hiking in the area. He directed me to one that is near a campsite in the park.

While riding through the area, I was able to find one true thong tree and one casualty. With the little research I had completed, it was easy to see the difference.

ROUTE:

From Woodall Mountain in MS: US-72 to Corinth. US-45 north to Jackson, TN. US-412 through Dyersburg to MO. I-155 to I-55 to SR72 which joins SR21 near Arcadia. Pick up Highway CC to the park (322).

SIDE TRIPS:

Union Electric's Nature Museum features Indian artifacts, wildlife, birds, wood products, geology of the area, and a model of their hydroelectric power plant on Proffit Mountain. Although the hydro plants have less generating capacity than the company's fossil fuel and nuclear plants, they provide a reliable and economical supply of electrical power. This Taum Sauk Plant is a pumped-storage facility located on Missouri Highway AA, eight miles north of Lesterville. Construction on the plant was begun in June 1960, and it went into commercial operation in December 1963. The $50,000,000 plant adds 350,000 kilowatts of capacity to the company's system.

This plant serves a special purpose in the generating capability of Union Electric. A variation of only five degrees of daytime summer temperature can cause an immediate increase in demand for electricity equal to the entire capacity of Taum Sauk. Therefore, it is used primarily on a reserve basis and is put into operation when the demand for electricity is greatest — during the warm summer days. It consists of four main elements: the upper reservoir atop Proffit Mountain, a 7,000-foot shaft and tunnel, a power house containing the two reversible pump-turbine units, and a lower reservoir formed by a dam across the east fork of the Black River.

During peak demand periods, water is released from the

upper reservoir, flows down the shaft and through the tunnel. As it passes through the powerhouse, the water spins turbines to generate the electricity and it is then retained in the lower reservoir.

At night and on weekends when electrical demand is lower, excess power available from other Union Electric plants is used to reverse the rotation of the generating units. Water is pumped back to the upper reservoir. This pumping cycle takes 9.5 hours and requires up to 400,000 kilowatts of power. So, for each three economical night kilowatt-hours used for pumping, two daytime kilowatt-hours are returned when they are much more valuable.

The operation of the plant is automatically controlled through the microwave system from the 100-mile distant control room of the Osage Hydroelectric Plant. Loading and unloading of the units is accomplished by remote control from the load dispatcher's office in St. Louis.

SOME THINGS TO PONDER:

Electricity may be the only product in the world that is ordered, made and delivered in a split second. It is produced at 10,000 to 20,000 volts, but to be sent long distances efficiently, the voltage must be increased from ten to 30 times. Transformers located at each plant step up the voltage, and the power is then transmitted along high voltage transmission lines to substations where it is stepped down to 12,000 volts. Before the customer can use it, the power is further stepped down to 120 or 240 volts by transformers. So when we flick on a switch, that electricity has already been a lot of places and had many changes.

#25

Magazine Mountain, Arkansas
(2,753 feet)

Supper in Paris with K. C.

MY DAY OF riding began at 6:15 am with perfect weather. The storms had passed, leaving the countryside freshly watered and smelling wonderful. The thermometer I had mounted in my dash read 77 degrees, the sun was on my back, and the nearly full moon was ahead slightly to my left. If there could be one bad thing about the morning, it would be the bright sunrise in both mirrors. These times go too quickly, so I intended to enjoy the morning as much as I could. I was not in a hurry since I had only 360 miles to log by late afternoon.

Before long I passed through Pine Bluff and hopped onto US160, which passes through some of Mark Twain National Forest. Beautiful scenery and a couple of deer that stayed along the roadside just before 8 am contributed to the enjoyment of the curvy and hilly road. My dad would say: "This is the day the Lord hath made, let us rejoice and be glad in it." How could anyone not enjoy such a perfect day?

From past experiences, which were reinforced by motorcycle safety classes, I had learned the importance of continued attention to riding because situations can change so quickly. Schneider teaches their drivers the Smith System as a defensive driving technique, while the Motorcycle Safety Foundation (MSF) teaches an acronym of SIPDE. Since I was first introduced to it, I have tried to use the SIPDE process in riding. *Scanning* for vital information, *Identifying* potential hazards, *Predicting* what might happen, *Deciding* which strategy best deals with the situation, and then *Executing* either an adjustment to speed, adjustment of position, or communicating. Before I had to deal with the hazard I encountered that morning, I became aware that many folks in this area allowed their dogs to run loose.

I almost hit one puppy that ran across the road in front of me. Since I was *scanning*, I saw him running from the yard ahead to my right. I *identified* the potential that as a pup it may not have learned the dangers of crossing the road, so I correctly *predicted* that it would not use caution crossing the road. I *decided* to slow. In the *execution* of my decision, I rolled off the throttle and applied the brakes. The pup went on to live one more crossing, but had I failed any of the five steps in the SIPDE process, it would have put a damper on the day — for the pup, its owner, and me.

At 8:15 am I stopped to offer assistance to an elderly lady at an intersection. She had a friend who was bringing a chain, thinking she had blown the head gasket.

Breakfast waited until about 10 am, when I arrived in Salem, Arkansas. With a full tummy and tank and an empty bladder, I was ready to enjoy SR9, which was another wonderful ride—I didn't use much of the center of my tire tread. I have often wondered if my tires would last longer if I lived where there were more curves so I could save the center of my tread, which seems to get used first.

That afternoon as I got to I-40 on SR9, I stopped to help a lady with three children. The accessory belt on her Toyota was gone! That meant the battery was not being charged and water was not being circulated. At least two lights should have warned her, but she drove until it was overheated. Her son, in his early teens, was opening the radiator cap as I drove up. The small explosion and spray of steam and boiling coolant was a big surprise to him, and he was lucky to not be burned badly. I was able to assess the problem and stop a man in a pickup who had a set of jumper cables. It seemed strange that her battery was too low to start it. Maybe she had run it down before I got there. We were only about 1/2 mile from a gas station, so I had her turn around and follow me to it.

Years ago gas stations were often called service stations because they *served* the motoring public. As is typical nowadays, they had no service bays nor could they provide any help. While I was inquiring about help, her car stopped again. She waited there while I went into town to look for someone who could help with a belt. I found a very busy muffler and air conditioning shop that would help if she could get her car there. They were too busy to send anyone out to help her. Back at the gas station, we got her another jump-start and she followed me into town to the gentlemen who could help more than I could. I had done all I could, so I was on my way again.

Jeri's involvement at home was again helpful in coordinating my next meeting at Magazine Mountain. I was greeted once again by someone I'd never met before in person, but who'd been a great help through correspondence. K. C. Priest had ridden up from Louisiana and was sitting on his 1986 Gold Wing Aspencade at the Cameron Bluff Campground entrance when I rolled up at 4:50 pm (just 10 minutes ahead of schedule). He had found shade, but it was still a hot sticky afternoon —about 96 degrees and incredibly humid.

After exchanging greetings, we rode into Paris, Arkansas for dinner at The Grapevine Restaurant, which had been recommended by the service station attendant in Paris. Asking the waitress for her meal recommendation is normally very beneficial, but on that day we must have caught her off guard.

It looked like nobody had ever asked this young lady for her opinion before. After a bit of encouragement, we did get some suggestions and placed our orders.

With full tummies and tanks, we returned to the mountain for some sightseeing. We took a few pictures of the sun(less)set, our bikes and each other. There was soooo much humidity that the sun appears in the photographs as a slightly brighter spot in the haze. We located the remains of a lodge built in the 1930s that burned down in 1971. We got back to our FREE camping after adding 43 miles to our odometers, and set up our tents before we headed for the summit. I also filled my jug with water so it would warm some for the sponge bath I was planning later that evening.

From the Cameron Bluff Campground entrance, an easy hike of about half a mile took us to the summit of Signal Hill, which is the highpoint of Magazine Mountain. Since it lies in the midst of trees, we didn't have a spectacular view. We had not been in a hurry to get to the summit, so by the time we arrived, I needed my flash attachment to get pictures. In addition to several other sections, the Magazine Hiking Trail extends about 11 miles from the highpoint to Cove Lake.

That night K. C. and I shared the campground with only one other couple who pulled in as we were putting up our tents. With their large camper and pickup they had almost as many sites to choose from as did we, but had to consider how they would turn around, etc.

When the couple had camped there on another occasion, a park ranger warned them of a bear frequenting the campsites at night to look for food. I honestly don't remember if they said it was a black bear or brown bear. Let me say I'm not prejudice — I didn't want either color visiting our campsite at night!

I had a close encounter with a bear when I was a teenager and that is enough to last a lifetime. Mom, Dad and I were camping in Yellowstone National Park back when it had more trees. We had been told what precautions to take to decrease the chance of problems with the bears. You do know not to feed them, right?

We were all in the 15-foot travel trailer when I decided to go outside. Some of the details are as clear as if it happened yesterday (except I'm not still shaking in my boots). The door to the trailer was on the shoulder side with its hinge forward. Dad had backed into our space, and the car may have still been attached. If not, the car was still up near the trailer tongue. I opened the door of the trailer, bounded down the one step, and hit the ground with intentions of going toward the front of the trailer. Not three feet from me was a bear. Opening the door almost into its face may have surprised it, or maybe it just wanted me to know who was intruding into whose domain. It stood tall, and I was back inside the trailer, probably not using the trailer step on my return trip.

On this trip I wasn't carrying food with me and neither was K. C., so we both hoped we had nothing to attract a bear. There were no showers, so I brushed my teeth and took a sponge bath with one of my bandanas before turning in for the night. The cheerful chirping of the night animals didn't keep me from my appointment with sleep nor did the humidity. It was probably a couple degrees cooler than in Paris, so even a few feet of elevation helped.

I'm not generally a worrier, so I didn't lie awake jumping at every little noise, but I was glad during the night that K. C. was in his tent just a loud whisper away. After settling into our tents about 10 pm and quickly going to sleep, I awoke to sounds of the biggest bear I could imagine. He was rummaging through the garbage cans, which are intended to keep animals out. I'm not sure, but wouldn't that tend to make the bear mad? I know how mad I get when I can't get food out of a vending machine. K. C. assured me it wasn't a bear at all, just a raccoon. So I went back to sleep.

Early residents planted orchards found on the mountain during the 1870s. At one time, there were three hotels on the mountain, but they were all destroyed by the mid-1930s. Magazine Mountain Lodge may still be located on older maps, but it was burned in February 1971, just 30 years after it was completed.

The federal government acquired the area in 1930s and constructed a lodge, cabins, amphitheater, campsites and picnic areas. Following the fire in 1971, the area deteriorated. By late 1987, interest increased to establish a state park with more adequate water supply, visitor center, amphitheater, eventually a new lodge, cabins and modern facilities. Subsequent to this trip, construction has begun with plans for expanded park improvements.

ROUTE:

From Taum Sauk Mountain in MO: Highway CC to SR21 to US-60 to SR19 to Thayer and into AR. SR9 (past I40) to Oopelo. SR154 to Danville. SR10 to Havana. SR309 about 3 miles. Turn left (W) on Forest Road 1606 2 miles to Cameron Bluff Campground (480).

#26

Driskill Mountain, Louisiana
(535 feet)

Today felt hotter than it was.

B Y CORRESPONDENCE, K. C. had warned me that traveling in
Arkansas and Louisiana at this time of the year was not very
enjoyable because of the high humidity. I wore my white
painter's pants for the 400 miles I had ridden the previous day
and for the 276 miles with him between Magazine and Driskill
Mountain. We were up about 6 am and on the road about 7 am.
When we stopped for breakfast at a mom and pop restaurant, I
ordered just pancakes and a large orange juice. I usually have
no problem eating a large meal, but those 'plattercakes' were so
large that I couldn't finish them. By the time we ended breakfast and were back on the road, it was already about 95 degrees.
We were in no real hurry, so we spent the day enjoying the
scenery, talking on our CBs and trying to be as cool as possible.

SR7 is another road on which to use the sides of the tire
treads. We stopped often for liquids and when we got into the
area of Driskill Mountain, I tried to call the owner of the property, Oscar Bowman, who owned the property as of April 1990
(318-263-9668). He would prefer that permission be obtained
to cross his property. My call was unanswered.

James C. Driskill first settled the land, claimed the mountain, and gave it his name in the 19th century.

K. C. and I arrived at the summit at 4:50 pm. Driskill Mountain is located about 60 miles east of Shreveport and approximately 10 miles south of Arcadia. It was discovered as the state's highpoint in 1942 or 1943 while surveyors made maps for the army maneuvers that were held in that area during World War II. One of those surveyors was Paul Zumwalt, who is still an active member of the Highpointers Club and author of *Fifty State Summits*. There is no USGS benchmark on the summit, but there is a marker about 25 yards north of the summit.

In the July 16, 1989 issue of the *Sunday Advocate*, Baton Rouge, Louisiana, Curt Taylor said, "To most locals, the mountain is just another hill in the boondocks. There are no roads to it and no signs pointing the way. Half the people in Arcadia don't even know where Driskill Mountain is. They couldn't come up here and put their foot on it. But they know it's around here, and they're proud of it."

After a few more pictures of each other at the summit and with our bikes, we got ready to part. K. C. was to return home at Bastrop, Louisiana, which was to the northeast. I was heading for the other side of Texas. The long, level, straight stretch of road that was ahead for the next day was the only part of this trip, which a former Sunday School teacher/ banker/friend said would take pleasure away from the whole trip. For two days I had been riding in humid 95-degree sunny weather and felt whipped. I needed a good rest if Texas would be as bad as David Myers thought.

Before parting, K. C. (also retired from the military) suggested that I try getting into the bachelor officer quarters (BAQ) at Barksdale Air Force Base. I didn't figure there was much chance of getting in, but it was along the way, so I decided to check. Before starting this trip, I had gone to Selfridge Air National Guard Base near our home to have a base decal put on our Gold Wing. I thought it might come in handy if I needed to get onto any military installation along the way.

ROUTE:

From Magazine Mountain in AR: SR309 to Havana. US-10 to Ola. SR7 almost to ElDorado. US-167 through Junction City/LA to Dubach. SR151 to Arcadia. SR147 to SR797 Right on SR797 4 miles to a T. Right on 507 1 mile to Mt. Zion Independent Presbyterian Church and cemetery on the right (276). Park in the church lot then walk north on the dirt road for about 1/4-mile to a gate. Beyond the gate, about 100 yards the road forks. We took the right fork as suggested by a sign high in a tree.

SIDE TRIPS:

In Mt. Lebanon (on SR 154 and 517) there is the Stagecoach Trail Museum which contains documents, antiques, farm equipment, handmade tools, a gristmill and blacksmith shop. The museum was free and open Friday-Sunday, 2 pm to 5 pm.

About 5 miles south of Mt. Lebanon or SR 154 is a granite marker where the notorious Bonnie and Clyde were ambushed and killed in 1934 by Texas Rangers and a sheriff's posse.

#27

Guadalupe Peak, Texas
(8,749 feet)

Early to bed, early to rise...

～へ～

WITHIN AN HOUR of the time K. C. and I parted company, I left I-20 at the exit for the Barksdale Air Force Base. As I pulled up to the gate, the sentry executed a sharp salute—as crisp as any Marine's salute, and waved me through, but I stopped to ask about the BOQ. She pointed straight ahead and indicated it would be on my left.

I parked in front of the BOQ and went in with my helmet in hand. Pulling out my wallet to present my DD Form 2 (retired identification card), I greeted the young man behind the desk and told him I am a retired warrant officer passing through the area and looking for a room in the BOQ.

After spending two days and one night in hot and humid weather, I was not willing to spend the night in my tent. If there were no rooms at the BOQ, I would press on until I found a reasonable motel. In no time at all, I was registered, given my key, and charged $10 for one night. Can't expect much for $10, right? WRONG!

My room was on the second floor and the opposite side of the parking lot, so I couldn't keep an eye on the bike. But that was okay. I was planning to sleep, not watch the Gold Wing, which was about to turn over 43,000 miles.

My home base for the night was air conditioned and had the normal amenities of TV, bed, desk, etc. It also had some things I wouldn't find in a motel. How about an ironing board, iron, microwave, coffee maker, refrigerator and a closet larger than the one my wife and I share at home! Recalling my days on temporary additional duty while in the Marine Corps, I knew these were almost necessities for the officer away from his regular duty station, but I didn't need them on this trip.

After calling Jeri, I set the alarm for 3 am and turned in early. My next day across Texas was planned, and I wanted an early start since the Guadalupe Mountains were about 700 miles from Shreveport, and I planned to spend the night in the park at the foothills.

When I opened the door to my BOQ room at about 3:20 am, my glasses instantly fogged over, and I couldn't see. That was okay since I didn't need them for walking and loading the bike. By the time I had the bike loaded, they would have to be warmed up to the ambient temperature of 85 degrees so the humidity wouldn't condense on the lenses.

At 3:30 am I left the parking lot. I filled the Wing with gas in Shreveport and got back on I-20. It wasn't long before it cooled to about 80 degrees, which was okay for traveling, but still a bit too humid to be perfect. The farther I got into Texas, the less humid it got. By mid-morning the temperature was back up to 90 degrees, but since it was much lower humidity, it was quite nice. There was an abundance of small white clouds in the early morning. Sometime during the morning, I took a couple of pictures to show David (Chapter 26). When I told him about my trip plans, his attention was drawn to the long stretch across Texas, so I wanted him to see what he was missing. I had set my throttle lock about 65 and started my stopwatch. After 1 hour, 32 minutes, and 50 seconds I had gone 100.3 miles (64.8 mph) without touching the throttle. One picture was my dashboard to show my speed (63 mph),

RPMs (2800), and the 90-degree temperature. As a bonus, he could see the remains of a large bug on the windshield just above the speedometer.

My second picture that morning, especially for my friend, was of the road ahead where it appears that even the telephone poles on my left would disappear into the little puddle of water on the horizon. There were no cars as far as I could see. The white fog lines at the edge of the road and the broken yellow centerline disappeared into the mirage of water on the road ahead. Because of the sky's reflection in the water, it would have been hard to tell where the road met the sky, except for the greenery on both sides of the road, which left a small notch in the horizon.

A service truck from a concrete company passed me somewhere around Dallas/Fort Worth, Texas, and almost immediately started moving right. I followed, instinctively, near his left tire track. I was glad I did when I discovered that he was moving right to avoid a dead 50-60 pound dog. Staying in a tire path of the vehicle immediately ahead may be a good idea when that vehicle obscures our view of the path ahead. We can't control when a passing vehicle will cut back in front of us and reduce our ability to scan 12-14 seconds ahead.

A fox crossed my path at 5 pm as I entered the Pine Springs campground, and a while later I saw a small buck deer. Camping is permitted all year on a first-come, first-serve basis at both the Pine Springs and nearby Dog Canyon campgrounds. Both have water, fully accessible restrooms, tables, and sites for tents and recreational vehicles.

I did make two mistakes at the end of this 13-hour day. I was low on fuel and had not eaten since lunch. Fortunately, lunch was at Pizza Hut, where I stopped to bulk up on carbohydrates. The park and nearby area offer no food or gasoline. I wanted both but did without either.

Whites City and Carlsbad, New Mexico, were 35 and 55 miles respectively to the northeast. I would be headed that way the next day. Other choices would be Salt Flat or Cornudas

115

to the west, but both were just a small dot on the map. Van Horn, Texas, which was about 60 miles south, would probably provide as many options as Carlsbad. Considering the round trip on top of the nearly 800 miles already that day, I decided I would relax until nightfall.

As I got farther into this trip, more people asked what was my favorite highpoint, but it was difficult to say. When the trip was over, I was able to say that Guadalupe Peak is among the few that were special for different reasons. The Texas highpoint was the first real climb where I felt that I needed the hiking boots I had brought along. It also followed one of the longest legs of the trip from Shreveport, Louisiana, to the campground at the base of the mountain.

Guadalupe Peak is located about 110 miles east of El Paso in Guadalupe Mountains National Park. The Guadalupe Peak Trail is well-established and does not require rock-climbing abilities. The 4.2-mile hike from the campground to the summit is rated as Class 1—strenuous by most because of the 3,000 foot gain of elevation.

The park's 80 miles of trails offer a wide range of opportunities for exploring the desert, canyons, and highlands of the Guadalupe Mountains. Hikers, as well as horseback riders, are welcome.

The trails vary greatly in length and difficulty, from short nature trails to all-day hikes, or even a longer trail for several days. Many of the trails, especially leading to the high country, are steep and rough. The canyon and other lowland trails are less strenuous.

Some trails are well-maintained and defined while others are primitive and simply marked with rock cairns. A topographic map is essential for long trips and is available at the park.

That evening before my hike, I found six possible hikers for an early morning attempt. I was in my tent about 9 pm and quickly fell asleep. Up by 6 am, I found that none of those six wanted to go to the summit.

I left the campground at 7:05 am with a father and son team after signing the hiker registration, but they stopped too often for me. When I noticed another hiker within sight and ahead, I said my farewells and continued. By the time I caught up to that hiker, I must have felt cocky because after a short talk, I pressed on alone. Before the summit I passed another pair of hikers and was the first to make the summit that morning, unless someone I did not see did not sign in at the summit.

Often I would pause and look up the mountainside. Sometimes the path was evident as a ledge along its face while other times I couldn't pick it out except for immediately ahead. The sky was such a dark blue that even at mid-morning the moon stood out like a white button on a powder-blue shirt.

I lost track of how many lizards I saw after counting about a dozen by halfway up. About 45 minutes before reaching the top there was a sign for a campground. One hiker said that it was about one mile from the summit.

Five minutes before I reached the monument and registered, I met a lady bug convention. Assuming they do not have a system for mass communication, why were they all there together? It appears that God doesn't give them a free will as he has given us.

At the summit is an impressive marker erected by American Airlines in 1958. There was very little breeze when I reached the summit at 9:45 am, and I had worked up a good sweat, so when the wind started about fifteen minutes later, it was a pleasant happening. Going back down requires less effort but inherently provides potential problems not encountered on the climb. Many hikers have lost toenails after similar descents by repeatedly jamming their toes into the front of their boots.

I was back to the parking lot by 11:45 am, had more water and began packing. I had made the trip to the summit with about half of the water recommended, but because I paced my drinking, I still had about 1/4 of the water I took up.

My trunk bag was a Christmas gift from Dennis and Keri Sutton, my brother-in-law and his wife. On the first day of the trip when I had some rough roads, the bag was tossed from the rack on my trunk, so I had been carrying it on the passenger seat most of the time. It was very hot by noon, so I put the trunk bag back on the rack, hoping it would allow a little more circulation of air around my lower back. I don't use a backrest, because I think it would be too warm on a day like that. Even when Jeri is with me on warm days, I don't like for her to have anything against my lower back for very long.

As with many American Indians, the Mescalero Apaches believed their gods dwelled on the summits. These peaks were skirted by the Butterfield stagecoach route and evidently contain no precious metals, but around 1900 a man named Long found a chest of gold coins in a cave in one of the canyons. He used his new found wealth to buy a ranch in cool, green Oregon.

Journey Into Summer by Edwin Way Teale, gives account of his 19,000-mile journey. In Chapter 11, called High Rocks, he introduces Mr. George H. Peters, who spent two decades of summer vacations traveling about 60,000 miles in pursuit of a prodigious hobby. He had ascended the highest points of 49 of the 50 states and had brought home from each summit a bit of rock. Labeled and dated, those high rocks were arranged on the shelves of a special oak cabinet at his home in Freeport, New York. Mr. Peters was a botanist and mountain climber from Long Island who visited most of these highpoints as early as the '30s and '40s. In the '90s many people would frown on taking a rock from our summits. It was interesting that his high rock from the highest point in Texas was white and filled with fossils of small sea creatures.

To me, this is just one more small piece of evidence to prove the Bible is true. God did flood the world by causing a 40-day rain and water to come up from the ground, which covered even the highest point in Texas that is now a mile and a half above the sea.

Others explain these fossils a different way. The U. S. Department of the Interior in the *Official Map and Guide* to the Guadalupe Mountains (reprinted in 1995) for example, explains the evidence of marine life a mile and a half above current sea level. Our Department of the Interior believes the Guadalupe Mountains are an "... extraordinary natural phenomenon, which formed about 250 million years ago." This was not the first time I ran across the 240-250 million year ago theory. But don't be surprised when you read on the Guadalupe Peak marker erected in 1963 that it was some 200 million years ago. That's allowing for a 25 percent error!

Their theory continues:

> During this time, a vast tropical ocean covered portions of Texas and New Mexico. Over millions of years, calcareous sponges, algae, and other lime-secreting marine organisms, along with lime precipitated from the seawater, built up to form the 400-mile-long, horseshoe-shaped Captain Reef.

> Eventually the sea evaporated. (Author's note: If it evaporated, that means all that water went into the air and stayed, or fell somewhere else). As the reef subsided, it was buried in a thick blanket of sediments and mineral salts. The reef was entombed for millions of years until a mountain-building uplift exposed part of it. This ancient reef complex now towers above the Texas desert in the Guadalupe Mountains. Other parts of the reef are exposed in the Apache Mountains and the Glass Mountains.

To believe that theory takes more faith than I have.

According to the same *Official Map and Guide* to the Guadalupe Mountains,

> Nde (Mescalero Apaches), westward-bound pioneers, explorers, stagecoach drivers, U. S. Army troops, ranchers, and conservationists are all part of the col-

orful history of Guadalupe Mountains. Until the mid-1800s, these remote highlands were the exclusive domain of Nde, who hunted and camped here. Later camp explorers and pioneers welcomed the imposing sight of the Guadalupe peaks rising boldly out of the Texas desert not only as an important landmark but also for the water and shelter the mountains provided.

But cultures conflicted and the Nde did not welcome the intrusion of new people into their domain. In 1849 the U. S. Army began a campaign against them that was to last three decades. The Guadalupes became the only sanctuary from the soldiers as well as a staging ground for their own attacks. By 1880 the last of the Nde had been driven out of the Guadalupes.

Amidst this conflict, Butterfield stagecoaches began carrying mail through the Guadalupes on the nation's first transcontinental mail route. The ruins of the Pinery stagecoach station are a reminder of this historic service.

In the years that followed, some ranching operations developed. One ranch in McKittrick Canyon was built in the 1930s and donated to the National Park Service in 1959. Additional land was purchased from J. C. Hunter, and in 1972 Guadalupe Mountains National Park was created by an act of congress.

The Chihuahuan Desert surrounds the Guadalupe Mountains and is sparsely populated. It extends south for hundreds of miles into Mexico and gets between 10 and 20 inches of rain a year. Summer temperatures rise to 90 degrees and above. Although it can look barren at first glance, the desert is full of life, but you are more likely to see it in the cooler evenings and mornings than during the heat of the day.

"The most beautiful spot in Texas" has been used to describe McKittrick Canyon, where the deep, sheer-sided walls form a showplace for an impressive diversity of plants and animals. Lying between the desert below and the highlands above, it has a mix of life that is part desert, part canyon woodland, and part highland forest.

The National Park Service provides a Headquarters Visitor Center. One can discover the desert as he walks from the visitor center to the ruins of the Pinery, a Butterfield Trail stagecoach station. The Pinery Trail is an easy, wheelchair-accessible, 3/4 mile round trip with trailside exhibits. It ends at the Pinery parking area on Highway 62/180.

ROUTE:
From Driskill Mtn. in LA: SR507 to SR797 to SR147 to Arcadia. I-20 through TX to Pecos (Exit 42). US-285 38 miles to Orla. CR652 US-62/180 to Pine Springs Campground (785)

SIDE TRIPS:
Carlsbad Caverns is located about 60 miles northeast of Guadalupe Peak. The big room is the world's largest underground chamber and these limestone caverns contain spectacular colorful stalactite and stalagmite formations. Which are which? The stala*ctite* hangs *tight* from the ceiling, so the other is the one on the floor of the cavern.

From the Pine Springs Campground, there are several other trails besides the Guadalupe Peak Trail. Here's a sample of what you can find:

The Devil's Hall Trail is a moderate and level but very rocky 4.2 mile round-trip. It includes a climb of the Hikers Staircase and Devil's Hall in the Pine Springs Canyon.

The Bowl is a strenuous 2,500 feet of elevation gain, 9.1-mile round trip through a conifer forest. This high country hike includes areas recovering from a wildland fire that occurred in 1990. The Bowl includes part of the Tejas Trail, Hunter Peak side trip, Bear Canyon Trail, and Frijole Trail.

The El Capitan Trail leads through Chihuahuan Desert to the base of El Capitan at the southern end of the Guadalupe Mountain range. The moderate 11.3-mile round trip includes the Salt Basin Overlook Trail and beyond the overlook, the trail continues to Williams Ranch, an additional 4.7 miles one-way.

There's even the Permian (Paleozoic) Reef Trail with a 2,000-foot elevation gain if you are interested in seeing what the water left behind.

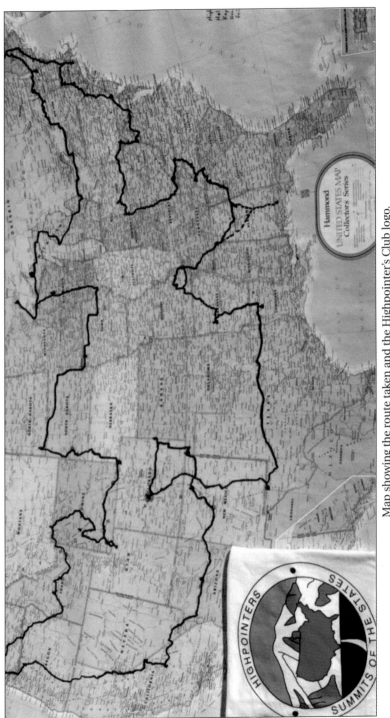

Map showing the route taken and the Highpointer's Club logo.

*If a picture is worth a thousand words,
Then a trip is worth a thousand pictures.*

Our youngest son, Jason, and his friend Brian Boers did not work on the Monday that I started this trip, so when they heard my departure was delayed, they decided to begin it with me. Just minutes after posing for this photo we were headed north, where I would cross into Canada on the Blue Water Bridge at Port Huron, Michigan.

At the end of my first day I checked into the KOA at Natural Bridge, New York, where I had my choice of sites. The excitement of the first day seemed to make the first 465 miles go by too quickly.

For my first highpoint (in New York) I arrived too late to make a safe hike to the summit so I hiked to Marcy Dam, which takes about 45 minutes, but I was gone almost two hours. A hike to the summit is a strenuos 7.4-mile hike, which makes for a long, arduous day.

Soon after rolling off the car ferry into Vermont my attention was drawn off the road to my right to a large black bear straddling a motorcycle in the middle of a garden. "That's what can happen to me on these curvy roads if I don't pay attention," I thought.

Mount Mansfield. Blazes are painted rectangles about 3" x 6" and mark the footpath along the trail. Cairns (rock piles) also mark the trail to help guide hikers in poor weather and/or visibility. Disturbing these trail markings may cause subsequent hikers significant problems, so please don't alter any blazes or cairns. Lives may be at stake!

My nephew Mike, his wife, Angie, and their son, Ian, were standing along the stone wall that surrounds the monument at High Point, New Jersey. They were enjoying the panoramic view of the countryside with Mara sitting on the top of the wall.

As we talked about years gone by, Mike made me feel old when he mentioned possible retirement from the Air Force in about three years. Could I be old enough to have a retired nephew? They were currently stationed at McGuire Air Force Base and made the trip just to meet me.

Although Ebright Azimuth is one of the lowest highpoints, it's actually unique since it's in a residential neighborhood.

One-sided "flag" red spruces, deformed by constant exposure to strong westerly winds, are seen from all four sides of the stone and steel observation tower, which sits atop Spruce Knob. The USGS benchmark is just north of the observation tower.

There are no plans to limit hiker access to Backbone Mountain's Hoye-Crest area (named after Captain Charles Hoye), but visitors are on private property.

Bernard Coffindaffer spent more than $2.5 million putting up sets of crosses after he had a vision following open-heart surgery that told him to start building *crosses of mercy*. Eventually some 1,800 were placed across twenty-nine states.

Campbell Hill is marked by a USGS benchmark embedded in concrete, flanked by brick, and twenty feet south of a flagpole on the property of Ohio Hi-Point Joint Vocational School. Howard Pletcher and I did not need permission to enter the property, but noticed a sign indicating the gate is not always open.

We missed the gravesite and birthplace of Annie Oakley because I talked Howard into going through Troy, Ohio instead. But he did take me for a walk along several preserved canal locks at Lockington.

Previously unnamed, Indiana's highpoint was named by the Indiana legislature in June 1993. Hoosier High Point is still often called Hoosier Hill—although that's not its name.

As I approached the summit of Black Mountain from SR160, I took the center of three paths about 150 yards past a large white FAA radar dome. I was able to ride to the tower and antennas located at the peak. The old tower would probably offer a spectacular view of the area, but the lower steps had been removed to discourage climbers.

It is unusual to observe the sun setting from Mount Mitchell. When I arrived at this drive-up highpoint located northeast of Asheville, even the park ranger was a bit wrapped up in the sight.

Visibility on the day I visited Clingmans Dome and the next two highpoints was not good. A local radio station reported record high pollution. It wasn't fog.

At Sassafras Mountain the parking lot is only about 100 yards from the summit marker, but as with a few other highpoints there is no view of the countryside.

With the unusual name of Brasstown Bald I expected to find an interesting story about how it received its name, but the story is a little confusing. The name of Georgia's high-point is derived from the Cherokee word meaning *new green place* or *place of fresh green.*

Cheaha State Park is an old-fashioned 2,719-acre piece of land that doesn't give you the feeling Holiday Inn arrived ahead of you. You'll want to visit the Civilian Conservation Corps Museum at Cheaha Mountain.

Previously owned by James and Dorothy Roe, the land surrounding this highpoint was purchased in July 1991 by the Missouri State Parks System. Along the edge of the parking lot are information boards and the beginning of a relatively new cement path.

K. C. Priest and I shared a site at the Cameron Bluff Campground with only one other couple who pulled in as we were putting up our tents. With their large camper and pick up they had almost as many sites to choose from as we did.

It was an easy half-mile hike to the summit of Signal Hill, the highpoint of Magazine Mountain. It lies in the midst of trees. We had not been in a hurry to reach the summit, so by the time we arrived I needed my flash attachment to take pictures.

Before leaving Driskill Mountain, K. C. suggested that I try getting into the Bachelor Office Quarters (BAQ) at Barksdale Air Force Base. That was well worth my effort. Thanks, K. C.

While crossing Texas it appeared that even the telephone poles would disappear, along with the white fog lines and the broken yellow centerline, into the mirage of water on the road ahead. Because of the sky's reflection in the water, it would have been hard to tell where the road met the sky, except for the greenery that left a small notch in the horizon.

Guadalupe Peak is among my favorite highpoints. This Texas highpoint was the first real climb where I felt that I needed my hiking boots and also followed one of the longest legs of the trip, from Shreveport, Louisiana to the campground at the base of the mountain. The ledge around the corner is much wider than it appears.

From Walsenburg, Colorado, be ready to enjoy some prime riding. I'm especially partial to riding alongside rivers.

It is not uncommon to find lakes near highpoints, as here at Colorado's highpoint, which was named in honor of the Territorial Governor Samuel Elbert (1833-1899), and the town of Elbert, Colorado.

Technical ability and special mountain climbing experience are not required to climb Mt. Elbert, but good physical condition is necessary. The ascent and return requires a fairly full day of strenuous hiking. What surprised me the most was not how quickly I was out of breath at the higher elevation. I expected that. But I did not expect to be able to catch my breath so quickly when I stopped along the trail.

Because of the Highpointers Konvention that weekend Bob Newson and I discovered a 60-person throng of hikers when we arrived at the top of Colorado.

The 11th Annual Konvention of the Highpointers Club was held on July 24-26, 1997 in Leadville, Colorado. Much of the Konvention is not structured so there's plenty of opportunity to meet new Highpointers, renew old acquaintances, and share pictures and stories with other Highpointers.

With my feet about four feet apart on either side of the Wing's opposed six-cylinder engine, I wasn't having much fun riding on loose gravel. I did want to reach Mount Sunflower, so I pressed on slowly for 3.5 miles until I came upon this sign.

Black Mesa is another special highpoint for me. It has this obelisk that was contributed by the *Tulsa Tribune* and includes several bits of information like: Cimarron County is the only one of America's 3,070 counties that touches as many as four states. The Indian Head Granite monument was quarried in Oklahoma and is about nine feet tall.

Leaving Albuquerque, New Mexico there were dark clouds as I passed a Harley rider under a bridge donning his rain gear. Within a couple of miles another Harley rider was along the shoulder, but he already had his gear on. When I stopped to offer help he asked if I saw his friend behind me. As I was telling him about the rider under the bridge, the first rider rode up. After a short chat I was invited to ride with them. I decided I would.

This *Snowbowl* ski area is about 10,000 feet and near Humphrey's Peak. A good trail exists for the 4.5-mile hike to the summit. I knew it would require more time than I had available, but a couple of years later Brian Boers and I did make it to the summit.

In 1864 Mount Whitney was named in honor of Josiah D. Whitney (1819-1896), who was the Chief of the State Geological Survey from its creation in 1860 to 1874. A geological expedition under the direction of Whitney first measured the height of Mount Whitney in 1864.

MT. WHITNEY
USC & GS EL= 14,494.164
FIRST ASCENT AUGUST 18, 1873, C. BEGOLE, J. LUCAS, A. JOHNSON

TRAIL MILEAGE AND ELEVATIONS	DISTANCE MILES	KM	ELEVATION FEET	METERS
WHITNEY PORTAL TRAIL HEAD	0	0	8,360	2,548
JOHN MUIR WILDERNESS SIGN	0.5	.8	8,500	2,591
LONE PINE LAKE	2.5	4.0	9,850	3,002
OUTPOST CAMP	3.5	5.6	10,365	3,159
MIRROR LAKE	4.0	6.4	10,640	3,243
TRAILSIDE MEADOW	5.0	8.1	11,395	3,473
TRAIL CAMP	6.0	9.6	12,000	3,658
TRAIL CREST	8.2	13.2	13,777	4,199
JOHN MUIR TRAIL	8.7	14.0	13,480	4,109
MOUNT MUIR	9.0	14.5	14,015	4,272
KEELER NEEDLE	10.2	16.4	14,000	4,267
MT. WHITNEY SUMMIT	10.7	17.22	14,494	4,417.83

King, for whom Kings Peak (Utah's highpoint) is named, made two attempts to be the first person to climb Mount Whitney; but he climbed the wrong mountain. Three fishermen, C. Begole, J. Lucas, and A. Johnson, were the first to reach the summit on August 18, 1873.

The precise location of the California-Nevada border in this area had a long and varied history that wasn't settled until 1980. A survey done in 1873 put Boundary Peak in California, but the U.S. Coast and Geodetic Survey between 1893 and 1899 placed the border far enough west to include the summit in Nevada. Why it took almost another 100 years to settle this issue becomes more understandable when you visit the area and see the terrane.

Mount Hood is a stratovolcano, a peak composed of loosely consolidated ash, pumice, and rock fragments inter-bedded with thin flows of lava and mud. Mount Hood was last active in August 1907.

The two-day visit with the Pitchers went too quickly. Our family met David, Pam, Crystal, and John in Hawaii just before I retired from the Marine Corps, but I had not met David's mother who was also there from out of town.

Birch Springs Road took me to the parking area from which the trail leads to the summit of Borah Peak.

While packing Thursday morning I began talking with Brad Tresek from Savage, Maryland who was loading his red Honda ST1100. Our conversation began with motorcycles, which led to a very interesting story about Moxie that is so typical of the friendships made when bikers meet.

Rick and Joyce Vandersloot from Wyoming's GWRRA Chapter C said that I should be sure to stop at the Farson Mercantile for a world famous ice cream cone. Gold Wing riders seldom miss an ice cream place.

Many peaks near Kings Peak are above 10,000 feet and seldom see 80 degrees, with nights often at 30 to 40 degrees, even during the warmest months, so from I-80 many snowfields can be seen on the slopes.

Claud Alden and Art Hendrickson discovered Panorama Point in 1951. The Kimball Chamber of Commerce erected this marker in 1971. The chamber office in Kimball will supply a map with clear directions to Panorama Point and the nearby Three-State corner marker, along with a certificate to commemorate your visit to Nebraska's high-point.

Within a mile of Panorama Point I stopped to get a closer look at thirty-eight bison from the H. P. Bison Ranch. Several appeared to be six feet tall. Since they often weigh 2,000 pounds and can run at thirty miles per hour I chose not to get very close.

Al and Lois Vogele are closest to their red Gold Wing that Al had converted to a Lehman Trike. John and Linda Lehman wave as John's brother-in-law Rennie Jensen searches for a light. Mr. Lehman has been making trike conversions since about 1987.

White Butte requires a hands-in-pocket hike of about two miles. Mrs. Angeline Buzalsky would prefer that permission is obtained before crossing her property (701-879-6370) and that you not disturb the Indian burial grounds on White Butte.

There is no USGS benchmark at Iowa's highpoint, but Mr. Sterler has placed his expired Iowa license plate "HIGHT PT" on the cattle-feeding trough. The Sterlers would prefer that permission be obtained to cross their property (712-754-2045). They welcome visitors and provide free key chains to those that visit.

In addition to a pair of lawn chairs at the summit I found the Charles Mound Guest Register with a written welcome from Wayne and Jean Wuebbels. When I visited Charles Mound, in addition to the signs identifying the highpoint, a number of other signs addressed the fact that Charles Mound was again for sale.

Price County purchased this land surrounding Timms Hill in 1978 and completed a county park in November 1982 that includes a metal tower over the USGS benchmark and another wooden one to climb.

The United States Department of Interior survey team, using aerial photographs and controlled benchmarks in 1961, found Eagle Mountain's elevation to be 2,301 feet making it Minnesota's highest point.

Although Dad was legally blind he still enjoyed comparing notes about cars as Brian, Roger, and Ted looked under the hood of the rented Cadillac.

We were gone from Dad and the vehicles for an hour and a half and never did find my last highpoint. I had been too confident and did not take to heart the warning: "Due to logging operations the roads in the Mount Arvon area are frequently changed." We gave up the quest at 8:15 p.m. and returned to L'Anse, picked up a cake, ice cream, and all the fixings for our birthday party back at the motel.

When the weather is good, having the headlights of family and friends shining in my mirrors, or following their taillights, makes a good ride GREAT.

<h1>#28</h1>

<h1>Mount Elbert, Colorado</h1>
(14,433 feet)

Location of the 1997 Highpointer's Konvention.

T HE 639-MILE TRIP from Guadalupe Peak required a stop en route to stay overnight since I left Texas about noon. Las Vegas, New Mexico, was along my route and had a KOA, so that's where I stopped for the night, long after the sun had set. By this time in the trip I needed almost no light to put up the tent. I was often given a choice of campsites, so I chose one next to a couple on a Harley. We didn't talk much that night since it was late, but in the morning I found out they had been traveling mostly by expressway from the East. The day before they had decided to begin taking more back roads as they continued their trip West.

At 1:50 pm I stopped to offer help to a family who had a flat tire. They appreciated the offer, but were about ready to be going again since they did have a good spare and jack and knew how to use them. They did make a point to say that I was the only one to stop. I often think it's a shame that we are too afraid or in too much of a hurry to stop and offer help to someone along the way.

The Highpointers Club 11th Annual Konvention was July

24-26 in Leadville, Colorado. Much of the Konvention is not structured so there's plenty of opportunity to meet new Highpointers, renew old acquaintances, and share pictures and stories with other Highpointers. This year, a group campsite was reserved near the trailhead so the cost per person was only $10 per night. Many others made reservations to stay in the nearby motels, inns and resorts from the list provided by those Highpointers who hosted the Konvention. The final event of the weekend was a banquet on Saturday night for just $25 per adult.

Leadville, Colorado, is an old mining town, the result of the gold and silver boom in the 1800s. It is the highest incorporated city in North America (elevation at one spot within the city limits is 10,430 feet). But don't be surprised if you hear that Alma (about 15 miles from Leadville) is the highest town in North America. These two lofty claims are the result of a fight for a title of height. Alma has a spot that is 10,578 feet, so how did these neighbors settle the fight for title of height? The residents of Alma, with a population of 160, proved to be sporting good neighbors by claiming only to be the *highest town*, which allows Leadville, with a population of 3,100, to lay claim to being the *highest city* in North America.

Abe Lee discovered gold in 1859 in an area near Leadville, which came to be known as California Gulch and produced $100 million in gold. As the gold began to play out, miners discovered the troublesome black sand they had been sifting through to reach the gold was laden with silver. Leadville was established in January 1878 and named for the source of the silver. Leadville was little more than a rough collection of log homes and small shops at first, but as the word got out about Leadville, thousands flocked to the city to claim their share of the riches. By the spring of 1879, more than 100 people were arriving every day. In 1880 the city boasted 30,000 residents including 61 doctors and 120 lawyers. The city had 18 bakeries and more than 100 saloons.

I arrived at the Lakeview Campground at 4:15 pm on

Friday, July 25th. Some of the Highpointers had already climbed to the summit. Others were planning a hike up on Saturday morning. I was almost five hours ahead of schedule, so I had more opportunity than I had thought I would have to prepare for the hike. I joined Dick Barthel, another Highpointer, to bulk-up with a pasta meal for supper. I also couldn't resist getting a few Snickers for some quick energy during the climb.

During my stay in the Leadville area, I made a note that nature is for us to enjoy, but it doesn't care about us. The Creator can also be enjoyable, and loves us so much He died for us. Do you worship/appreciate the Creator or His creation?

Colorado's highpoint might best be viewed from US 24 between Leadville and Granite. It was named for Territorial Governor Samuel Elbert (1833-1899). He was an outstanding and widely known civic leader in the territory and state of Colorado. Mt. Elbert, Elbert County, and the town of Elbert, Colorado, were all named in his honor. Elbert served as Colorado's territorial secretary, territorial governor, and state supreme court justice. He was active in the formulation of mining legislation and reclamation projects as he promoted concepts of conservation and irrigation, which were ahead of his time.

The first recorded trip to the summit of Mt. Elbert was made by H. W. Stuckle, but as it is with other states, another mountain, Mt. Massive, was thought to be the highest peak in Colorado at 14,368 feet for many years.

I rode to the 4x4 parking area just up from the campground with Bob Newson. I first met Bob at the Highpointers Annual Konvention in Minnesota in 1996 before I became a member. That year we rode together to the trail head, hiked together, shared a table at the banquet on Saturday night and even bumped into each other the next day in Michigan as we each tried to get another highpoint on our way home. He was returning from the summit of Mt. Arvon as I was going up. This time, Bob headed for the 4x4 parking area by turning about one mile past the Lakeview Campground on SR82, just several yards past the overlook turnout on a dirt road suitable for 4x4's but not well suited for Gold Wings or other large touring bikes.

We left Bob's rented four-wheel drive at 6:35 am and arrived at the summit four hours later. Because of the Highpointers Konvention that weekend, the top of Colorado was cluttered with hikers—between 60 and 70 at our pre-noon arrival.

It took two and a half hours to get down and it started raining just a half-hour before I got back to the car. That reinforced the general guideline I had heard to get off the mountains by noon since there are often afternoon showers and thunderstorms.

Technical ability and special mountain climbing experience is not required to climb Mt. Elbert, but good physical condition is necessary. The ascent and return requires a fairly full day of strenuous hiking. What surprised me most was not how quickly I was out of breath at the higher elevation—I expected that. But I did not expect to be able to catch my breath so quickly when I stopped along the trail. Altitude can affect even the healthiest people with headaches, dizziness, and nausea, so if you feel these symptoms, get down to a lower elevation immediately. (See chapter 36 about altitude sickness). Have water and food for quick energy.

Since this was my longest hike, I would like to include some things hikers can do to protect the peaks and help maintain the challenge of climbing for others. Serious erosion and vegetation damage in the fragile alpine environments is becoming evident with the growing popularity of highpointing, peak-bagging and mountain climbing.

- Travel on designated trails whenever possible, even when they are wet or muddy.

- If you must travel cross-country, do so on rock, talus or gravel as opposed to tundra soil and vegetation. Cutting straight up a slope leads to severe erosion.

- Avoid descending slopes that can set off slides and rock falls. Be aware of climbers below you.

- Be considerate of your fellow hikers and campers. Some are there for the solitude experience.

- Avoid building fires except in designated places.

- Don't build rock structures on mountain peaks or destroy existing structures, which may be culturally significant.

- Don't leave flags or other objects on the peaks. Many peaks have registers to record your visit — please leave them.

- Watch wildlife from a distance rather than try to get too close, which may disturb their normal routine.

- Turn back at the first signs of lightning. Watch for building clouds but don't wait for lightning to strike before turning around. Being off the peak by early afternoon is a good general guide.

- Be prepared for any type of weather. Carry proper rain gear and extra layers of warm clothing. Not having proper clothing can lead to hypothermia, a lowering of body temperature.

- Be aware of the signs and symptoms of altitude sickness. Dizziness and nausea are symptoms that should tell a person to get down to lower elevations as quickly as possible.

- Carry the essential supplies for survival and first aid. Know the basics of first aid, especially for hypothermia.

- Carry a topographic map and a compass and know how to use them.

- Let someone know of your plans, including your expected time of return. Then remember to check back with them when you get back.

⚓ Some summits are crowded on weekends, especially holiday weekends, so if you enjoy solitude, plan your trip during the week.

You will find that Mt. Elbert is a popular climb. The two traditional routes, the Mt. Elbert Trail and the Northeast Ridge, get crowded on weekends and holidays. Trail markings can be confusing so study ahead of time whenever you plan one of the longer hikes. The little time you spend in preparation will almost always pay dividends later. Books might soon become out of date, which makes the newsletters from the Highpointers Club one of your most valuable sources for recent changes.

If you are a golfer you may want to try golfing at some of the high-elevation golf courses. Since the air is thinner up there, the ball is slowed less by the air. At 10,000 feet you will probably experience a 10-15 percent increase in your drive — and even a greater increase in your ego! To fellow golfers who slept through physics, you can brag about your longer drives while getting extra exercise highpointing.

You likely will not see motorcycles around Mt. Elbert when 100 snowshoers compete in the 15-mile Elbert Ascent Snowshoe Challenge each February, but one would expect some such event when you learn that Leadville is the snowshoe capital of the world. They host six very challenging (and fun) races in the Leadville Snowshoe Series each year.

ROUTE:

From Guadalupe Peak in TX: US-62/US-180 to Carlsbad, NM. US-285 through Roswell to Vaughn. US-54 to Pastura. SR219 to US-84 to Las Vegas. I-25 through Raton to Walsenburg, Colorado. From here on, be ready to enjoy some very wonderful riding. I'm especially partial to the portion of riding along a river. SR69 (5 miles past Hillside) to CR1A to Cotopaxi. US-50 to Salida. SR291(Oak St) 9 miles to US285 to Johnson Village. US-24 toward Leadville, CO. 15 miles before Leadville I went west on SR82 about 4 miles to the Lakeview Campground (639) which is on the north side of the road.

SIDE TRIPS:

Highpointer and motorcyclist Mike Bromberg suggested that I go to the top of Cottonwood Pass, at 12,126 feet near Buena Vista. This gives one of the best views of the Colorado peaks. The 30-mile round trip is on a new and excellent road, which allows riding up to the top at a good speed.

The National Mining Hall of Fame & Museum will help you begin to understand and appreciate the rich heritage and excitement of the American mining industry.

#29

Mount Sunflower, Kansas
(4,039 feet)

An easy highpoint is not always easy.

AN AFTERNOON OF rest was in order following my decent from Mt. Elbert, which ended with rain. By the time of the Konvention banquet in Frisco, Colorado, at the Holiday Inn, I was showered and rested. The most dressed up I could get was a pair of clean jeans and matching vest that announced my membership with GWRRA and CMA while posting about a dozen of my latest pins and patches, but that was not a problem. Most dressed casually for the banquet. The Saturday evening meal, program and meeting were a wonderful end to a great Konvention.

Sunday provided another day of rest. I was the first one to arrive in the church parking lot of the First Baptist Church of Leadville, which claims to be America's highest baptist church. There we go, another lofty claim!

I don't generally like to do things like washing on Sundays, but on this trip that was my plan. After church and lunch, I spent a couple hours at the Leadville Laundromat. Some young ladies were there from California to get acclimated to the thinner air and ready for a race the following week.

After adding 86 miles to my trip by riding around Leadville during my stay at the Twin Lakes Campground, I was awake before 6 am and departed at 6:40 am into a damp 55-degree morning. I had filled with fuel Sunday evening before I turned in for the night, so my tank was almost full. It wasn't until 8:20 am that I saw my first glimpse of the sun. My windshield was dry for only about five miles of my first hour and a half.

Colorado Springs was about 125 miles from my campsite, so I still had almost a half tank of fuel. Passing through without stopping for fuel turned out to cause me anxiety before long. In Colorado Springs I joined up with a few Gold Wing riders also headed east. The one immediately ahead had an Ohio license. I never did talk with them because I had my 3-in-1 portable CB packed away. Once through town, they continued on US-24, but I left them to cut across SR94.

As the fuel gauge needle got closer to empty, I saw Rush on the map about 33 miles ahead. Since I often listen to Rush Limbaugh, I thought it would be memorable to fill with fuel in Rush. The first of the problems when I arrived in Rush was that I found no gas stations. Decisions, decisions, decisions. I didn't recall seeing a filling station in Yoder or Ellicott during the past 16 miles. From previous experience, I remembered there was no station ahead of me in Punkin Center. Jeri and I had stopped there the previous year to take a photo since we have always called our oldest son Punkin. If I were going to make it 22 miles to Punkin Center and another 32 miles to Aroya, I would need to maximize my MPG.

I started driving slower and watched as the needle entered the red-lined empty mark on my fuel gauge. There was nothing in Aroya or Wild Horse, so it was on to Kit Carson another 20 miles past Aroya. By then, I was sure I would be pushing it to the station. I had filled with fuel Sunday evening and ridden to the campground before I started this leg of the trip. When I got to Aroya and onto US-40, I had already gone 232 miles since I filled with gas. Could I make it 252 miles on a tank or gas? I didn't know.

As I approached Kit Carson, the evidence of a gas station on the horizon was a more welcome sight than a friendly face in a strange place. The trusty steed only took 5.509 gallons so it wasn't quite empty (the owner's manual says it's a 6.1-gallon tank). I regained my composure by having a sub and juice before continuing to Mt. Sunflower in Kansas. As with Britton Hill in Florida, this would normally be an easy highpoint to bag. But just as with Britton Hill, I was prevented by bad weather from reaching the summit here also.

As I crossed into Kansas on US40, I noted the odometer so I would know which gravel road to take north. Just as planned, I headed north on the gravel road 1.5 miles from the state line. A small sign on the northeast corner assured me that I was on the right road to Mt. Sunflower. The gravel was loose and evidently had recently been plowed. It was like riding in snow and reminded me of the first time I rode in snow and slush on a Gold Wing. I had gone to Macomb Community College to teach an experienced riders course on our 1984 Gold Wing. The morning rain turned to freezing rain and then snow by the time we finished our morning classroom work. When it was time to go to the range, we had at least an inch of snow on the wet ice. Most of the students left their bikes at the college when we were forced to cancel the class.

Before my 15th birthday, I learned to ride a motor scooter in the snow and on the ice while delivering the *Detroit News* on my paper route. Rather than leave our Gold Wing at the college, I decided to ride home. It would be about 18 miles. If there were no other vehicles on the road it would be less of a problem, but with paths in the snow, the bike's tires get a notion to follow a car tire track from time to time. On a smaller bike it can be fun riding in the snow, but I was not having much fun on the Gold Wing in the snow until I arrived safely at home without dropping it.

As I continued slowly on the snow-like sandy gravel, I used the technique learned as a youth. With legs ahead and almost straight, if the Wing began to tilt one way because the tires

132

were sliding the other way, my leg would act like the pole of a pole vaulter and help upright the bike as that foot made contact with the road.

With my feet about four feet apart and on either side of the Wing's opposed six-cylinder engine, I wasn't having much fun riding on the loose gravel. I did want to reach the summit, so I pressed on slowly for 3.5 miles until I came upon a sign: *ROAD CLOSED.*

I couldn't see the problem so I continued until I went over the next rise. From there I could see the flooded roadway ahead. I had listened to weather stations as a truck driver and was immediately reminded of their service announcements advising that we not drive through a flooded road. With all the difficulty I was having on dry sand, I did not desire to attempt a wet and maybe washed-out sandy road so I turned back for US40, figuring that I did get within ten miles of the summit, but never saw it.

A welded metal sunflower greets visitors reaching the summit of Mt. Sunflower, which is located on property owned by Ed and Cindy Harold. Highpointer Rick Peterson, who lives in Kansas, loved the comments in the register about altitude sickness, forgetting ropes, ice axes, crampons, etc. and visited this highpoint twice while picking up his 48 peaks. It may be a joke to a lot of people, but many more make the trip from other states to record their visit in a registry, which is kept in the mailbox at the summit. Cindy said that visitations totaled 500 ten years earlier. That number increases with each new year. Any guesses about how many visited Mt. Sunflower in 1997? I wasn't one of them.

ROUTE:

From Mt. Elbert in CO: I took US-24 through Colorado Springs (which included a ride over Wilkerson Pass at 9507 feet with great views, even in the rain!) SR94 to Aroya. US-40 to KS. US-40 1.5 miles (276). North on gravel road 11 miles. Left on another gravel road where the sign indicates Mt. Sunflower.

Go 1 mile to a fence on the right running N-S with a gate near the road. Mt. Sunflower is in sight to the N. Turn right and continue through the gate and N across the pasture for less than 1/2 mile.

#30

Black Mesa, Oklahoma
(4,973 feet)

If you see no roses to smell,
take time read the registers.

I'M EXCITED TO KNOW that the Highpointers Konvention will be here in 2002. This was one of my favorite highpoints, so I will do by best to be here during the gathering July 24-27, 2002.

Although the effects of bad weather had prevented me from getting to Mt. Sunflower, the day was great for riding to and from Kansas. While heading south on US-385, I stopped to offer help to a stranded trucker. He said that five hours earlier he had sent for help. As we talked, his tow truck arrived, so I got back underway. It was 214 miles from my turnaround point near Mt. Sunflower to the Black Mesa State Park, where I arrived at 5 pm and pitched my tent for the night. Total miles for the day was right at 500. This was one of a few places where cows had free access to the roadway. They didn't move as quickly as deer, but they are bigger, so I gave them lots of room and slowed down.

I was a bit ahead of schedule when I chose my spot from more than 150 campsites. I took some time to look around this park, which was established in 1959. There was no place close to buy a meal. The park has 33 RV sites with electric and water hook-ups and 22 picnic tables, some with cookout grills for day use.

Most of these picnic tables are enclosed or covered to provide some protection from the sun and rain. For those with many followers, there is a group picnic pavilion that accommodates 20 people and is equipped with water, an electrical outlet, and cookout grill. I doubt that many of us could fill the group camps 12 bunkhouses which accommodate 132 overnight guests and include a fully-equipped kitchen and dining hall plus a bathhouse with hot showers. But the Highpointers Club will probably fill to overflowing when they hold the 2002 Konvention here in July. Expect pre-convention activities starting on the 24th with the official convention beginning on Friday evening and ending with a banquet on the Saturday evening of July 27th.

Before sunset, the sky got unusually dark not an uncommon event in the Southwest. Like the oldies song says, there was nowhere to run, baby, nowhere to hide. A storm was rolling in, and I decided to ride it out inside my tent. Before the rain started falling, the wind blew. The sides of my tent popped in the strong wind, reminding me of the sounds I used to make with towels when Mom wasnt around. When the rain started, the wind calmed a bit.

I was warm when I woke in the night, but wet. The rain, which made its way into my tent and collected on the floor, had been soaked up by my sleeping bag. Only a small portion of the bag needed to be off my air mattress to act like a sponge and mop up the water. By morning my tent was dry on the outside. The mornings weather report informed listeners that I had survived 3/4 of an inch of rain. I packed and left camp at 7:15 am with the temperature at 67 degrees.

When I arrived at the parking lot to begin my hike, it was almost 8 am and I was well into a beautiful morning for the eight-mile round-trip hike. Hiking boots were a real plus for this hike, though comfortable riding boots would suffice.

Having just experienced a downpour, I wanted to be back from the Mesa before noon, so I hiked up at a good clip. I arrived at the granite monument on the Black Mesa summit at 9:35 am. Although much of what I read cautioned about rattlesnakes, I neither saw nor heard any. I must have been making enough noise in my quick pace that they heard me coming.

The current obelisk (monument) was contributed by the *Tulsa Tribune* and includes several bits of information like: "Cimarron County is the only one of America's 3,070 Counties that touches as many as four states." The Indian Head Granite monument was quarried in Oklahoma and is about nine feet tall.

I saw a photograph of Truman and O. W. (his father) Tucker being helped by at least two other men when they hauled the original monument onto the highpoint in 1928. According to locals, Truman was still living in the area (born about 1905).

No trip to this area would be complete without a stop at the Kenton Mercantile, which was founded in 1898 and known as Lord's Store in 1910. On the shelves are bones, teeth, and other evidences of long ago. I hadn't eaten for about 24 hours, so I requested a burger, which the young lady did a fine job of preparing in the small area set aside for food preparation. It may not have been the only place to eat out in Kenton, but even if there had been another choice I would have eaten at the Mercantile.

Although my time was short, I did choose to meet two more of the 42 residents of Kenton. LaVerne Hanners and her son grew up in the area, and she has written a book that includes the history of the area. Her book tells about the Panhandle being annexed to Oklahoma in 1890 and the outlaws who found this area to be a safe haven in the late 1800s. She is an expert on the events of the area.

Black Mesa gets its name from the thick layer of black rock, which caps the mesa (table). The region contains the fossilized remains of dinosaurs and archeological evidence that

Native American farmers inhabited the region before the more recent Plains Indians who were primarily nomadic hunters who roamed the southern Great Plains in pursuit of bison or buffalo.

According to an undated *Black Mesa State Park/Nature Preserve* flyer, Spanish explorers, including Coronado, crossed this region in the 1500s. The historic Santa Fe Trail crossed near Black Mesa as an important trade route linkng the U.S. with north Mexico. Kit Carson was among the frontiersmen who used this trail from 1821 until 1880 and established Fort Nichols on the trail for security from Plains Indians who aggressively defended their homeland against outside intruders. The remains of the fort are now on private land, but access to the fort and other attractions, which are on private land in this area, might be granted with help of the Boise City Chamber of Commerce.

On January 17, 1991 the Nature Conservancy took title to 1,500 acres of the Black Mesa when they purchased the property from Texas rancher Ed Smith. Ed and his wife Betty had owned the property since 1986.

As with many other summits, there was a notebook at the summit for visitors to record their visit. What do people write? You name it! A few visitors write things not worth reading, let alone sharing, but some like Laurie Smith record their impressions for others to read. I don't think she would mind if I shared her note written on June 1, 1997:

> Words are hard to dig up when trying to express your feelings of this beautiful sight! I think that the phrase "God is an awesome God" can do the trick! We have had a lot of good experiences — some that we can take down from the mountain. I've learned tolerance, patience, and especially perseverance! I've made many new friendships and deepened the ones I already had. I hope to come back soon and experience more of the same stuff...even more! Psalms 121.

ROUTE:

From Mt. Sunflower in KS: Backtrack on gravel roads about 13 miles to US-40 west to Cheyenne Wells. US-385 south to OK where it becomes SR3 to Boise City. SR325 for 35 miles. Right on blacktop road marked Colorado (which is 6/10 mile before the Kenton Mercantile.) 5 miles to the preserve parking area on the west side of the road (258).

SIDE TRIP:

The Kenton Mercantile is a must.

#31

Wheeler Peak, New Mexico
(13,161 feet)

Whom do you believe?

WITH A FULL TANK of fuel from the Kenton Mercantile, I left that little historic town of 42 residents at 2 pm and headed west into a very dark horizon. My route carried me near, but not into, the afternoon storm. I decided not to put on my rain gear since the temperature was a comfortable 80 degrees. A downpour and a ten-degree drop in the temperature would be more enjoyable than riding very long at 80 degrees with a rain suit on.

At 3:50 pm I offered to help a young couple with children. As with several other situations, I wondered if they needed help but were afraid of taking it from a motorcyclist. Some people are like that, you know! The young man said they needed no help; they were letting the engine cool. I question whether on not that helps — unless the radiator is low on water or the thermostat was stuck closed. Instructions from Schneider National, for whom I drive a truck, tell drivers to allow the truck to idle a few minutes to cool after highway driving. Turning off the engine and stopping along the road means the water no longer circulates. The heat in the engine cools only to the point it heats the water therein—often beyond the boiling point. If the vehicle is driven at a moderate speed or idled with a cooling fan operating, the water is allowed to cool in the radiator, then circulate into the heated engine to cool the engine block. Anyway, my offer to help was refused and I was on my way again.

Having missed the afternoon thunderstorm, I made it to Taos by 6:15 pm, which was 210 miles from Black Mesa in Oklahoma. Wheeler Peak is located in north central New Mexico and was named in honor of Major George Montague Wheeler. For ten years he led a party of surveyors and naturalists who collected data in New Mexico and six other Southwestern states.

A section of the Taos Ski Valley has designated parking for hikers near the Twining Forest Campground. Two basic choices of hikes to the summit exist. The longest route is about 14 miles round-trip and may be a gentler climb. The more direct hike along Lake Fork to Williams Lake is a little more than eight miles but includes some cross-country hiking. Both routes are Class 1, strenuous hikes at high elevations, so acclimation to thin air is important.

Reported elevation gains and distances of hikes often differ among sources, which is one reason for not including many of those details in this book. Here, for example, I found three reliable sources with different information on the longer trail. The round-trip distance was reported as 13.6 miles to 14.4 miles with elevation gains reported between 3,761 feet and 4,700 feet. One author, at 66 years old, made the round trip in less than nine and a half hours, but another recommend as many as 16 hours for the trip.

I had not planned a hike to the summit here. To spend most of a day here would not allow me to get to Washington by the weekend, and I wanted to spend Sunday with long-time friends there. As it turned out, the weather did not cooperate anyway. Around Taos I was in and out of sunshine, sprinkles and fog.

There is a metal plaque and summit register atop a three-foot monument at the highpoint as well as a USGS bench-mark. I was not satisfied with information of when the dedica-tory monument and plaque were placed on the summit of Wheeler Peak, New Mexico (maybe 1969). And the year of Wheeler's birth and death may be wrong on the plaque, which says 1832-1909. One report said that George Montague Wheeler was born in 1842 (not 1832) and died in 1905 (not 1909). The contrary author said Wheeler was born October 9 in Grafton, MA, and graduated sixth in his class in 1866 from West Point. Wheeler retired in 1888 and was in New York, New York, when he died May 5, 1905.

This writer had even more details, which seemed to add creditability to his claim. He said the Wheeler survey was offi-cially titled: *Geographical Survey of the Territory of the United States West of the 100th Meridian.* Determination of altitude was always a weakness of the 19th century. The atmospheric barometer had been used with some success from the early 1800s. Wheeler's survey teams used the more sophisticated and accurate aneroid barometer; even so, their altitude mea-surements were frequently off the mark by hundreds of feet. The Wheeler Survey was discontinued in 1879 though it was more than 1/3 completed. Congress had voted to abolish all surveys and established the U. S. Geological Survey.

ROUTE:

From Black Mesa in OK: Backtrack through Kenton on SR325 to SR406 through Seneca to US-56/64. Stay with US-56 to Springer then take I-25 to Exit 419. SR58 to Cimarron. US-64 to Eagle Nest. SR38 to Questa, then SR522 for about 10 miles for the road to Valdez (210) where the Taos Ski Area is located.

SIDE TRIPS:

Taos Pueblo, near Taos, has been continuously inhabited since about 1200 AD, and is one of the premiere Indian Pueblos in the Southwest because it is very similar today to what it has been for hundreds of years. It is just ten miles from Taos and the $5 entrance fee is worth it. There is an additional cost for using your camera, but no Indian pueblo is as photogenic according to fellow GWRRA member L. Deane Crawforth, who has learned much about New Mexico since his move there many years ago.

Deane also recommends a trip to Cimarron, which gives one a real taste of the Old West, complete with the 1872 St. James Hotel, inside of which 16 men were shot. Famous guests include Clay Allison, Billy the Kid, Bat Masterson, Black Jack Ketchum, Buffalo Bill, and Jessie James. There is a museum in the old mill with fascinating memorabilia.

#32

Humphreys Peak, Arizona
(12,633 feet)

Becoming a tag-along.

F EW MOTORCYCLISTS enjoy riding into and out of rain and fog, especially in unfamiliar territory, but my senses were alive with all that was stimulating them as I watched Taos in my rear view mirrors. It took nothing more than my nose to know that God had just taken dust from the atmosphere, mixed it with hydrogen and oxygen, and washed the countryside clean. Was it the excitement of the moments or the rapidly falling temperature as night engulfed that high elevation that reminded me to look up the verses in Job 37?

"...(God) thundereth with the voice of His Excellency; ...God thundereth marvellously with His voice; great things doeth He, which we cannot comprehend. For (God) saith to the snow, Be thou on the earth; likewise to the small rain, and to the great rain of His strength... By the breath of God frost is given... stand still, and consider the wondrous works of God" (Job 37:4-14 KJV).

About a year earlier *Wing World* had published my request that asked for some help with planning, executing and writing a book about this trip. I was about to meet one more of a few who was a great help. "How much help?" you may ask. His first of several letters was seven typed pages plus maps, etc.

L. Dean Crawforth lives with his wife Diane in Albuquerque, which is 140 miles from my last highpoint. I placed a call to confirm that I was about on schedule and headed their way, and he gave me directions to find them. Although Diane only rarely rides with Dean, she does encourage him to get out and ride because she knows how much he enjoys it. But I'm not sure Dean is the type of guy who needs to be encouraged to ride. During my stay with them for the night, I saw that we were similar in more than just that way.

Although a trip from Albuquerque to Madison, Wisconsin, would normally only involve five or six other states and a round-trip distance of about 2,600 miles, Dean went through 15 states and covered 4,700 miles during his trip to Wisconsin for Wing Ding in 1996. Did he get lost a lot? Of course not, he just likes to make the best of an already good situation. I told you that we were similar!

Dean is an electronic engineer with a varied career as an engineer and manager in communications equipment design, development, manufacturing, quality control and application. At the time of my visit he had been working with a consulting group, which allowed him to have a flexible schedule.

At Dean's suggestion, after leaving their home the next morning, I stopped along I-40 adjacent to the San Jose de la Laguna Mission and took a picture. Signs along the pull-off area explained some of the history this way:

> This picturesque mission church of San Jose de la Laguna was built around 1706 by Fray Antonio Miranda and shows the single-isle floor plan commonly used in pueblo churches. It has been repaired many times and acquired its distinctive white stucco exterior in 1977. The church contains a beautiful and well preserved alter screen made between 1800 and 1808 by a folk artist known only as the 'Laguna Santero.' The interior walls are mud-plastered and

whitewashed and the floor is made of packed earth. The handsome wooden ceiling is laid in a herringbone pattern.

I soon came upon a Harley rider along the road. No problem, he was just under a bridge donning his rain gear. Ahead was a very dark sky but I chose to ride on without rain gear. Within a couple miles another Harley rider was along the shoulder but he already had his gear on. When I stopped to offer help, he asked if I saw his friend behind me. As I was telling him of the rider under the bridge, the first rider rolled up. After a short chat, I was invited to ride with them and decided I would.

About ten miles down the road I saw a third Harley rider who was watching traffic from an exit ramp. Within another mile, he passed me at the back of the trio of bikes and slid into the number two position. Some people are not shy about joining other groups, I thought. This was neat; we were starting a motorcycle convoy. When we did stop later, I found out that these three were traveling together from the South Bend, Indiana, area. Doug, Ray and George were headed for Sturgis, South Dakota. I-40 through Albuquerque, New Mexico, can be along the route when traveling by motorcycle. (Remember Dean's trip to Madison?)

We rode together most of the day, which included a brief stop at the Painted Desert Visitor Center in Arizona. A 20-minute film at the center showed how our Eastern Shore was once joined to our neighbors across the Atlantic Ocean. Most geologists before the 1960s were adamant that continents were stationary, but that has changed. They have been slow to accept the account of how God created our universe, but they are gradually finding the truth of Genesis. According to that film, about 225 million years ago our continents began drifting apart, leaving an ocean between. The current theory that incorporates seafloor spreading and continental drift is known as "plate tectonics," but the film at the visitor center showed a slow and gradual spreading of the seafloor as the only explanation of this change. Our National Park Service will not even present the *catastrophic plate tectonics* of Dr. John Baumgardner, which is able to explain more geological data than the slow and gradual spreading theory. According to Genesis 1:9-13, God spoke dry land into existence during the third day of His creation when He gathered the waters together. Dr Baumgardner, using supercomputers to model a rapid process, has been acknowledged for developing the world's best 3-D supercomputer model of plate tectonics, but our National Park Service doesn't even mention it to visitors. They continue to present the lopsided picture that everything just happened during the past millions (or billions) of years. The magnetic pattern in the volcanic rock formed on the sea floor at the mid-ocean ridges is just one piece of geological data that suggests a very rapid spreading process.

After leaving the visitor center, we all filled with fuel and got in line to ride through the Painted Desert. Before long, I got out of line and said my goodbyes to Doug, Ray and George. I didn't really want to spend so much money to ride through.

About a half-hour down the road I observed three bikes in my mirrors, closing quickly. When alone, I usually set the throttle lock about 60 mph. When they passed me, doing the speed limit, I increased my speed to ride again with the same three guys. I found out later that they also decided the Painted Desert ride was not a priority.

As our motorcycle quartet pulled into Flagstaff, Arizona, we filled with fuel and sought out the visitor's center. After gathering information for our respective trips, I asked one of the gentlemen behind the counter, if he had a friend in town just for the night, where he would take him to eat? Without any hesitation he referred us to *The Horsemen Lodge*. Then he handed us flyers of the restaurant, which claimed to be *where Flagstaff goes for supper*.

One of that evening's specials was buffalo. I don't remember who of the other guys had tried it once before, but I decided I would. I was not dissatisfied. The half-inch slice covered most of the platter and was covered with peppers, mushrooms, and onions. I'll not go farther, in the event that you are trying to diet. We left pleasantly stuffed and they were ready to settle in for the night, but I pressed on toward Humphreys Peak.

I drove the paved road up to the ski area *Snowbowl*, which is at about 10,000 feet. A good trail exists for hikes to the summit, but I knew it would require more time than I had available. The hike is 4.5 miles each way, Class 1, moderate with a 3,150-feet gain in elevation. A couple of years later, Brian Boers and I did make it to the summit, but not on this trip.

The peak was named for General A. A. Humphreys who was the U. S. Chief of Engineers. From the summit on a clear day, the higher rim of the north side of the Grand Canyon can be seen to the northwest. To the west is Kendrich Peak at 10,418 feet. To the south can be seen the Red Rock Canyon of the Sedona area. As it is with other Native Americans living near great mountains, many Navajo, Hopi, and some Anasay in this area worship Humphreys Peak

ROUTE:

From Wheeler Peak in NM: SR150 to Taos, SR68 to US-84/US-285 to I-25 to I-40 to Flagstaff, AZ. Exit 201 to US-89 to US-180 to Snow Bowl Road. Follow the Snow Bowl Rd 7 miles to Snow Bowl (507).

#33

Mount Whitney, California
(14,494 feet)

The Lord's righteousness is like the
great mountains.

Aﬀter Humphreys Peak, I continued only a short time before stopping in Williams, Arizona. The sky to the west was dark and threatening so I decided to stop early. By 8:45 pm, I was checked into my room. Ahead was Death Valley, and I didn't want to be there in the hottest part of the day, so I was up at 4 am. A cool 50-degree calm but damp air surrounded me as I left the comfort of my motel room. I fueled the Wing and had an apple juice before hitting the Interstate at 4:30 am. By 7 am the temperature was already up to 80 degrees as I made my way through Kingman, heading for Las Vegas and Death Valley.

Just before leaving US95 heading for Death Valley Junction on SR373, I met a couple in Amargosa Valley who should have difficulty sleeping at night. Gas at their station was $1.999 (average for this trip was $1.257). The drinking water in their little store was even more expensive than their gas, and I was a little sick to my stomach to see how they took advantage of a busload of foreign tourists who stopped. Not knowing when I might see another gas station, I topped off my tank but made a special point to get the last little bit from the pump. Jason, our youngest son, had showed me how to get an extra half-cup of fuel by turning off the pump, when so equipped, then squeezing the handle lever again. The last bit of fuel doesn't register on the pump. Later he pointed out to me that it does-n't affect the station's profitability. In essence it takes a little from the next customer. Shucks, the next customer was already paying more than is just, and I made it worse for them!

At the visitor center within Death Valley, gas was only $1.76, so don't stop in Amargosa Valley. I entered California at 10:43 am, which was much later than I had hoped, but the temperature was only 95 degrees. That's not bad in the desert since there is very little humidity, but the fact that I had to pay another $5 to drive 147 miles through Death Valley National Monument got me hotter under the collar than the sun beating down on the desert floor.

According to Don W. Holmes, in his book *Highpoints of the United States*, Clarence King, a member of the Whitney survey team, named Mt. Whitney in 1864 in honor of Josiah D. Whitney (1819-1896). Whitney was the chief of the State Geological Survey from its creation in 1860 to 1874. A geological expedition under the direction of Whitney first measured the height of Mt. Whitney in 1864. King, for whom Kings Peak (Utah's highpoint) is named, made two attempts to be the first to climb Mt. Whitney but climbed the wrong mountain. Three fishermen, C. Begole, J. Lucas, and A. Johnson were the first to reach the summit on August 18, 1873.

The small stone hut near the summit was built in 1909 by the Smithsonian Institution. It was used from 1909 to 1913 to shelter scientists who made observations on the summit. The summit of Mt. Whitney is the southern terminus of the 210-mile long John Muir Trail, which extends north to Happy Isles in Yosemite Valley. This trail was completed in 1938.

As reported in the *LA Times* of July 20, 1989, Hulda Crooks climbed Mt. Whitney 24 times from age 66 to 91. The hike is a strenuous Class 1 with a gain of about 6,134 feet in just a little less than 11 miles of hiking. At 95 years of age she was strapped into the seat of an Army Chinook helicopter for a surprise. The chopper landed at a trail camp about 2,000 feet below the Whitney peak. A hiking party of friends and family met her as she received an honor granted to hardly anyone while still alive. Her grandson Bruce Couch, great grandson Patrick, and many friends stood as U.S. Rep. Jerry Lewis (R-Redlands) began to read a proclamation declaring that the second peak south of Mt. Whitney "shall be known and designated as Crooks Peak". Letters from President George Bush, former President Ronald Reagan and Governor Pete Wilson praised "the first lady of Mt. Whitney" for not only highlighting the importance of physical fitness for all Americans but also serving as a role model for senior citizens everywhere. It took five years to pass the legislation because congress was reluctant to honor someone still alive, Lewis said. Rep. Lewis removed his jacket and sweatshirt to reveal a blue Crooks Peak T-shirt and presented one to Hulda. After the applause subsided, she began to speak calmly and clearly.

> You know the Bible said the Lord's righteousness is like the great mountains. There is no limit to it. I give credit to my faith in the Lord that I've been able to survive so many years. What credit people try to give to me, I turn right over to the Lord. It's never too late to change your lifestyle if you realize it's not appropriate.

This from a woman who began hiking at age 66 after her husband died.

ROUTE:

From Humphreys Peak in AZ: Snowbowl Rd to US-180 to US-89A to Flagstaff. I-40 to Kingman. US-93 to Boulder City, NV. US-95 to Amargosa Valley. SR373 to Death Valley Jct. SR190 to SR136 through Keeler to Lone Pine. Whitney Portal Road 13 miles to Whitney Portal (540).

SIDE TRIPS:

The Interagency Visitors Center is one mile south of Lone Pine (US-395 & SR-136 intersection) and provides information on the surrounding area. They display color photography, drawings, minerals, books for sale, and give the latest weather and road conditions. At Independence, the Eastern California Museum has a Paiute-Shoshone basketry exhibit and presents the story of Manzanar, the Japanese-American WWII Internment Center. There are five acres of farm implements used by early settlers and equipment used during the construction of the Los Angeles Aqueduct (1908-1913). The highest and lowest elevations in the 48 contiguous states are both in Inyo County, only 80 miles apart. Badwater in Death Valley, 282 feet below sea level, is only two hours east of Lone Pine, and en route are old mining towns, Keeler and Darwin. Darwin has a museum with many old mining artifacts. Danti's View Point (5,475 feet) boasts the unforgettable view of the lowest and highest points of the 48 states. About 60 miles southeast of Furnace Creek Visitor Center, Tecopa has free hot baths at Tecopa Hot Springs and is open 24 hours per day.

#34

Boundary Peak, Nevada
(13,140 feet)

I couldn't find the sign.

I STARTED MY descent from Mt. Whitney at 3:45 pm to pick up US-395 north to Big Pine, California. What an enjoyable ride! The map shows that stretch of US-395 to divide two sections of the Inyo National Forest. It is also not very far from a part of the Pacific Crest National Scenic Trail, where the trail runs near the eastern border of the Kings Canyon National Park.

Boundary Peak is located at the northern end of the White Mountains, which encompass the Ancient Bristlecone Pine Forest. Established in 1958, the Ancient Bristlecone Pine Forest contains the world's oldest living trees, the Great Basin Prosecuting Pines, *Pinus Longaeva.* According to Don W. Holmes, in his book *Highpoints of the United States*, some of the trees are well over 4,000 years old.

At Big Pine the route got even better as I headed northeast on SR168. I started to wonder if SR168 from Big Pine to the Nevada border could be called the Deals Gap of the West. Deals Gap is along the North Carolina and Tennessee border at the western end of the Great Smoky Mountains National Park and just south of Bunker Hill. Deals Gap boasts 318 curves in 11 miles.

Signs along SR168 warned of no services for many miles, and the road narrows to one lane through the rock. The coarse blacktop was perfect for the roller coaster-like ride. Near the California/Nevada border, SR168 ended, and I headed north on SR264. As one might anticipate, the road became straighter since it travels in the direction of the mountains rather than crossing them like the stretch from Big Pine to the border.

I was supposed to be able to turn left, between mile marker 19 and 20, onto a dirt road. I was looking for, but did not find, a sign for Middle Creek and Trail Canyon. Instead, I saw signs for Chiatoyich Creek, private property, no dumping, permanently closed, and use south dump, but I wasn't too disappointed since I did not have sufficient time to attempt a climb to the summit on this trip anyway. The hike to the summit of Boundary Peak is a strenuous, Class 2 hike with 4,400 feet of elevation gain in four miles.

The precise location of the California/Nevada border in this area had a long and varied history that wasn't settled until 1980. According to Don W. Holmes, in his book *Highpoints of the United States,* a survey done in 1873 by Alexis Von Schmidt between Lake Tahoe and the Colorado River put Boundary Peak in California. But the U.S. Coast and Geodetic Survey between 1893 and 1899 placed the border far enough west to include the summit in Nevada. Why it would take about a hundred years to settle this issue becomes more understandable when you visit the area and see the terrane.

ROUTE:

From Mt. Whitney in CA: Whitney Portal Road to Lone Pine. US-395 to Big Pine. SR168 through Deep Springs. Pick up SR264 in NV and continue through Dyer. Turn left at a dirt road (between mileposts 19 & 20) with a small sign reading *Middle Creek, Trail Canyon* (127). Stay on main trail 7 miles to "Y." Go right toward Trail Canyon 5 miles bearing left 1 mile to the end of the road in Trail Canyon.

#35

Mount Hood, Oregon
(11,239 feet)

Stratovolcano, inactive since 1907.

S INCE IT WAS almost sunset and too late to attempt a climb
to the summit, I left the Boundary Peak turn-off area, heading
back into California via US-6. Seven miles past the California/
Nevada border, I took SR120 along the edge of the Inyo
National Forest. SR120 provided a roller coaster-like ride. It
could provide a lot of excitement at higher speeds, but I don't
generally enjoy pushing the envelope. Being unfamiliar with
the road, having no spotter ahead, and running the possibility
of wild life using the road, I suppressed the urge to run that
stretch over the posted speed limit.

Speaking of safety, I have some advice for passengers in
vehicles with passenger-side air bags. Since air bags inflate so
quickly, think about what happens to things resting on the
dash over the air bag. Hospitals are reporting numerous face
injuries when knees are forced into the passenger's face at
about 200 mph because their feet were resting on the dash
when the air bag was deployed.

Mt. Hood is a Class 4, strenuous hike of four miles with a
5,300-foot gain in elevation that should not be attempted

during the warm months of summer. One person described that a climb attempt in warm summer months would be like trying to climb a large pile of broken asphalt.

When Paul Lindsay completed his final summit of the 48 contiguous highpoints, he shared a word of caution in the *A to Z Newsletter* of the third quarter 1996. "Many of us have seen and felt what others hardly know exists. To me there is a friendship with the mountains that has a special spell. Some seem to say, 'Come join me and climb upon my angled back, but on my terms!'"

On October 29, 1792, Lieutenant William Broughton, a member of Captain George Vancouver's British expedition to the Northwest, sighted and named Mt. Hood in honor of Rear Admiral Samuel Hood, an officer in the British Admiralty. Mt. Hood is reported to be the most frequently climbed glaciated peak in North America. The best time to climb is not during the summer months, so my climb to its summit had to wait until another time.

Timberline Lodge was built between 1935-37 from native materials — stone from quarries nearby and giant hand-hewn timbers from the forests below. What began as a Roosevelt-era works progress administration project has become a unique National Historic Landmark. Mt. Hood has an information center about 15 miles west of Government Camp on US-26.

Mt. Hood is a stratovolcano, a peak composed of loosely consolidated ash, pumice and rock fragments inter-bedded with thin flows of lava and mud. Mt. Hood was last active in August 1907.

ROUTE:

From Boundary Peak in NV: Backtrack to SR264 to US-6 to CA and Benton. SR120 to US-395 to NV. US-395 to CA and Valley Falls, OR. SR31 to La Pine. US-97 to Madras. US-26 ALMOST to Government Camp. Right onto Timberline Rd to the Timberline Lodge (738).

#36

Mount Rainier, Washington
(14,410 feet)

That's it on the back cover.

FOLLOWING A 738-MILE leg of the trip from Boundary Peak to Mt. Hood, the 294-mile leg leading from Mt. Hood to Mt. Rainier seemed very short. In fact, it was shortened by a stop in Steilacoom, Washington. I was well ahead of schedule and looking forward to spending some time with David & Pam Pitcher, who are friends we made while I was stationed in Hawaii several years earlier.

I called late in the evening after leaving Portland. Pam gave directions to find them over the phone and I rolled in Friday evening at 11:30 pm. I had left Carson City, Nevada, about 16 hours earlier and was ready for a break, but I also wanted to visit. The two-day visit went too quickly with David, Pam, Crystal and John, but did include some activities before I resumed my quest for highpoints. David's mother was also there from out of town, so I got to meet her for the first time.

Saturday provided a good opportunity to change my engine oil for the second time during the trip. Saturday evening we enjoyed *Jesus of Nazareth,* presented at the Amphitheater in Puyallup, Washington, where their son John had a part. David was ushering that evening, and we had seats on the second or third row in the center to experience the 16th season of the life and ministry of Jesus. I often felt like we were right in the middle of the event since things were often happening to our right and left with nearly 180 degrees of viewing. My emotions ran back and forth from laughter to tears, anger to love, a desire to seek revenge to a better understanding of forgiveness.

Because of numerous responsibilities at church on Sunday, the family of four, with two houseguests, went to church in two cars at different times. It's always encouraging to experience first-hand the ministry in which our friends serve. I never knew that David played the violin. After church Sunday morning, we rested, did a little sight seeing and general "hanging out." We stopped somewhere along the water for pizza. None of us felt comfortable with the dark, smoky atmosphere inside, so we ordered the pizza to go and we found a couple of cement picnic tables nearby.

I left the Pitcher's on Monday at 7:45 am with wonderful weather, then stopped at McChord AFB to get fuel and more film. It was 11:00 am when I arrived in Paradise with a 70-degree temperature. Since I had washed and waxed the Wing during my visit with the Pitchers, it was ready for some "book-cover photos." Using my tripod, I took several shots along the road with Mt. Rainier in the background. There's one on the back cover, and it has not been altered. Standing along the roadside, it was as difficult to see where the snow ended and the cloud started just as it is in the photographs.

Mt. Rainier requires an eight-mile, Class 4 strenuous hike with a gain of 9,100 feet, so it is usually climbed during a two-day trip. Most climbing injuries and deaths on Mt. Rainier result from inexperienced and ill-equipped climbers getting hit by falling rock, ice, or snow, falling down steep slopes or into crevasses or becoming disoriented due to poor weather condition. Even the slightest climbing injury can result in tragedy due to the mountain's cold temperatures, high winds, and rapidly changing weather conditions.

Before the arrival of European explorers, Indian tribes lived in the lowlands surrounding Mt. Rainier. Some tribes called the mountain *Takhoma*, others *Tahoma*, meaning high mountain, great snowy peak, or just the mountain. On May 8, 1792, Captain George Vancouver, in command of a British government expedition exploring the northwest coast, named the mount in honor of his friend, British Rear Admiral Peter Rainier, so its name has nothing to do with all the rain you may encounter in the area.

Much like Mt. St. Helens, Mt. Rainier is a volcano that is believed to be dormant and not extinct, so, quite conceivably, it could one day erupt as did Mt. St. Helens. During the winter of 1971-72, more than 93 feet of snow fell at the Paradise weather station, but annual average is only about 52 feet. Nature hikes for people of all ages and abilities are available with evening and campfire programs. A museum at Longmire features geology, natural history, early exploration and the part Native Indians played in our past.

According to *The Story of Mount Rainier* by Mary Jacobs, Rear Admiral Peter Rainier very possibly did not even see his namesake. Other lords of the British Admiralty, Baker and Hood, were likewise honored by Captain Vancouver.

In his book *Mount Rainier*, Edmond S. Meany recorded details about the few men who accompanied Lt. August Kautz in 1857 to make the earliest recorded climb. Mountain climbing was hardly a sport in their day. What drew Kautz to the summit was probably the same prevailing passion we have today for going to the tops of high places. His group included two other soldiers, an Irishman, a German, and a doctor who reportedly filled his water flask with whiskey. They made crampons by sewing on an extra sole, through which were driven nails with the heads between the soles, and carried just one blanket each. They took a piece of ash with an iron-point called an alpenstock, to be their staff, a 50-foot rope, hatchet, thermometer (for calculating altitude), 24 hard biscuits and dried beef. Laugh if you wish, but many today try a climb on a nice day with less preparation and gear, but they soon learn the folly of such.

The Kautz' party started on horseback from Tacoma, 60 miles from the mountain, then continued on foot through dense underbrush and dark forests. Hunger, cold, thirst, insects, scratches and cuts plagued the party from its start. Sickness and weakness lingered for months after their return. There is doubt that Kautz found the actual summit, but he did make it to the crest and certainly deserves much credit for a very gallant effort. His own conclusions sum up his opinion:

> We are not likely to have any competitors in this attempt to explore the summit of Mt. Rainier. When the locomotive is heard in that region someday, when American enterprise has established an ice-cream saloon at the foot of the glacier, and sherry cobblers may be had at twenty-five cents halfway up to the top of the mountain, attempts to ascend that magnificent snow peak will be quite frequent. But many a long year will pass away before roads are sufficiently good to induce anyone to do what we did in the summer of 1857.

A few years later in 1870, a party led by General Hazard Stevens and Philemon Beecher Van Trump was the first recorded party to attain the true summit of Mt. Rainier. The other two climbers were Sluiskin, the Indian guide, and Edward Coleman, who had hiked in Switzerland. Their trip was full of toil and difficulty. They encountered waist deep rivers, ankle deep sand, dense jungles, fallen trees, swarms of gnats and mosquitoes, rockslides, avalanches and a shortage of water.

The Indian Sluiskin led the way. He had frequently hunted mountain sheep upon the snowfields but considered an ascent to the summit to be impossible. He claimed Takhoma

(Rainier) was an enchanted mountain, inhabited by an evil spirit who dwelt in a fiery lake on its summit. No human could ascend Takhoma and survive. Moreover, he claimed a furious tempest continually swept the crown of the mountain, which would tear the climber from the mountain and whirl him through the air by this fearful blast. He never the less agreed to lead the way.

During the first day of snow, Coleman, carrying the bacon, got stuck and had to throw away his pack to free himself. Then he returned to camp, leaving Stevens and Van Trump to attempt the summit alone. With their homemade snow spikes, alpine staffs, a rope, an ice axe, a brass plate inscribed with their names, gloves, and green goggles, the two climbers toiled for three more days over glaciers; loose, broken and falling rock; and overhanging deep, terrible gorges. More unremitting toil brought them to the middle peak of the mountain thoroughly fatigued and chilled by the cold, bitter gale. As it was late in the day, they were obligated to pass the night on the summit without shelter or food, except for their meager lunch. They found some shelter from the winds and used heat jets of sulfur through the night.

On the way down Van Trump had a bad fall. A three-day storm accompanied their remaining descent. The Indian returned to remove the injured Van Trump by horse and thus brought the triumphant climbers back from their adventure. It had been a long trip when they returned to the streets of Olympia by horse-wagon. Looking like long-time prisoners of war, their lean and gaunt bodies were evidence that a climb up Mt. Rainier was not to be taken lightly.

In the 1990s basic climbs begin typically from Paradise Lodge on the southern flank to Camp Muir and the Ingraham Glacier route in a two-day, eight-mile climb, gaining about 9,000 vertical feet. It is recommended that a guide be taken from Rainier Mountaineering Inc., (RMI) their offices are located at Paradise and Tacoma, Washington. A climber has approximately a one in four chance of successfully climbing

Mt. Rainier, with weather being a big determining factor, to say nothing of the premonitions of the Old Indian Sluiskin's evil spirits. A Mt. Rainier climb is an extremely serious adventure, not to be attempted by any other than very fit and well-prepared climbers with good leadership.

Altitude Sickness is a unique illness that may strike when we ascend to heights at which our lungs and circulatory systems are not accustomed. Flatlanders going up to 8,000 feet may quickly feel the affects of altitude because their bodies seem most accustomed to sea level. As we reach about 8,000 feet, we begin to feel a change in the atmosphere. Although the air always includes about 20 percent oxygen, higher elevations have less air and so there is less oxygen. Initially one might notice a slight difficulty breathing and, if unaware of the reason, that triggers anxiety. The anxiety causes more problems like trying to breathe faster, which may lead to hyperventilation. It can be scary if you don't know what's wrong. Problems with low oxygen are most acute for people who have gained altitude quickly. Within a couple of days, most people's bodies begin to deal with having less oxygen and either acclimate or don't acclimate and develop sickness. People with lung or heart problems must be especially cautious.

Acute altitude (mountain) sickness is marked by headache, nausea and vomiting, fatigue, malaise, swelling of hands or feet, drowsiness and frequent yawning, even depression and forgetfulness, and of course, shortness of breath. It usually improves in a few days or at a lower elevation. Knowledge, preventive measures, and being in good condition cannot completely protect us from altitude sickness, but all three will help. The purpose here is to make you aware of the need to learn more, for I am far from an authority on the illness. I have never experienced altitude sickness, but once observed it in my friend Brain Boers.

Whether you are in good condition should be obvious — the more able you are to run, climb stairs, pull & push with your arms, do sit-ups and other strenuous exercises, the better your condition. That leaves only preventative measures. Educate yourself, exercise a lot, drink plenty of fluids, eat complex carbohydrates and little meat or fat, and stay away from alcohol, tobacco and sedatives. If all this fails, listen to your body. God gave us wonderful things — pain, discomfort, thirst, etc. Without them how would we know to remove the stone from our boot or our hand from a hot engine part? If you begin experiencing symptoms, slow down your action and drink plenty of fluids.

Sleeping it off is not the answer. In sleep, we breathe more slowly, depriving our body of what it is lacking — oxygen. Disturbed sleep is common with altitude sickness, which might be God-designed so our bodies will rouse in an attempt to get deeper breaths. God is so caring! This is nothing to be macho about. Really bad things like pulmonary edema can happen. It may look funny to be mentally confused, stagger as though drunk, be incoherent or even hallucinate, but medical help is obviously needed at this point. Listen to your wonderful God-designed body!

ROUTE:

From Mt. Hood in OR: Timberline Rd to Government Camp. If I were not visiting friends in Steilacoom, Washington, I would have backtracked on US-26 to SR35 toward Hood River. From there I would have taken SR141 to Trout Lake and continue to Randle located on US-12 to SR706 to Paradise. Instead, I took US-26 through Gresham to I-205 and I-5 to Steilacoom. SR7 to Elbe and SR706 to Paradise (294).

SIDE TRIPS:

Paradise Inn was completed in 1917 and is now a National Historic Landmark. It was built to withstand heavy winter snowfalls of up to 25 feet.

At the Sunrise Chinook Pass you can find the Tipsoo Lake Picnic area and nave another good look at Mt. Rainier.

#37

Borah Peak, Idaho
(12,662 feet)

The USA is growing by 1/2 inch each year.

I LEFT MT. RAINIER Monday afternoon and, before going very far, I saw a vehicle on the shoulder of I-84. As was my commitment from before the trip, I stopped to offer help. The young man said their car just died. We both looked for any problems like a broken wire or hose, but after seeing none he tried starting it again. It started. To this day, I don't know why it stopped running. I followed the family of four along I84 until they exited to Pendleton, Oregon.

Within a few miles I stopped again to offer help to a young couple who was along the road with a blowout. They had a good spare, which they had just mounted and were repacking their car. With a good spare and a little effort, almost any driver is able to change a tire, and not be dependent on others for that minor inconvenience. It is much different when a motorcyclist gets a flat! Fortunately, when tires are properly maintained, blowouts are very rare on a motorcycle.

Between LaGrande and Baker City, Oregon, I stopped at one of the rest areas along I-84 to place a phone call. Ed & Terrell Pinson live in Boise, Idaho, and had written in response to my request for help as published in *Wing World*. Ed was thinking about going to Sturgis, South Dakota, about the time I was scheduled to be en route to Borah Peak, but he gave me his phone number and said to put it someplace handy and call him.

The pay phone was being used at the rest area, so I waited nearby with my notebook in hand. A couple about my age arrived with a younger woman and a wheelchair-bound older woman. Without staring, I noticed much love among the three as they all helped with the wheelchair trip to the restrooms and back to the car. They must have thought it odd that a guy would have a white three-ring binder in hand while waiting for the phone. Curiosity got the best of them, and we started talking. This would likely be their last stop before arriving at their destination. The younger woman was the daughter, who taught at a school in Kalamazoo, Michigan, and the wheelchair-bound woman was their 92-year-old aunt.

As they asked about my trip, I shared about a recent development at home. Jeri was trying to help a young couple who had just recently started attending our church. At the time I didn't even remember his name, but Brian had an injury on the job about a year earlier and was still having difficulty with blood clots and was unable to work. When the aunt was back in the car, she watched as the four of us held hands in the rest area and the three of them prayed for Brian, his wife, their three girls, and the help that Jeri was trying to give. Then I prayed for the Larson family, their love for the Lord, and asked traveling mercies for the remainder of their trip. Mrs. Larson reminded me of the fascination with high places as recorded in the Old Testament and commented that so many New-Age people are moving into higher elevations in Colorado. I made a note to do some research.

The first reference I found in the Bible with regard to high places and worship was in Genesis 22, when God told Abraham to offer his son as a burnt offering upon one of the mountains in the land of Moriah. That ended up being just a test of Abraham's faith and willingness to obey God so Isaac was not sacrificed. The second reference to worshiping in high places was when Jacob offered sacrifices on Mt. Gilead as a part of mending a relationship with his father-in-law. Before long, high places were often used as a place to worship idols of other gods and the quest continues today.

The phone was available when the Larsons left, so I placed the call to Ed & Terrell. Terrell answered since Ed had left her behind while he was off to Sturgis with a CMA friend. We agreed to meet for breakfast in Boise, then I headed to the Ontario State Park located just outside Ontario, Oregon, where I spent the night.

The Ontario State Park, as well as others at which I had stopped, used volunteer campers to register guests and do limited upkeep of the park. Evidently campers who volunteer for a period of time are scheduled and given free camping space for the time they meet their assigned responsibilities. I camped adjacent to the camp hosts who were in the first spot inside the camping area.

Following a delightful meeting at The Flying J with Terrell for breakfast, I was on my way out of town on one of my favorite types of roads—along a river.

Borah Peak is about 20 miles northwest of the USFS Ranger Station in Mackay, Idaho. Primary access is from US93. In error, I headed east on Double Springs Road, which is two miles north of Birch Springs Road. The 2.5-mile ride out Double Springs Road was a worthwhile, unplanned side-trip. Only three picnic tables and three signs were near a small parking lot just before a big dry ditch. The signs about the earthquake, event and results tell an interesting story.

EARTHQUAKE! *The Stage.* Idaho is part of the World's largest mountain chain above sea level. This chain extends from the tip of South America to Alaska's north coast. The widest section is in the Western United States — from the Sierra Nevada to the Rocky Mountains. The Lost River Range is one of the many smaller mountain ranges between the Rockies and the Sierra Nevadas.

The earth's crust, between the Sierra Nevada and Rocky Mountians, including the Great Basin, is stretching about 1/2 inch per year. And, it's getting thinner. Ever so often — a few hundred to a few thousand years — the crust breaks along the old fracture lines know as "faults." The valleys drop and the mountains rise, creating the 'basin and range' landscape you see from here.

The Event. There are no records from explorer journals or pioneers memories of earthquakes occurring in this area. Scientists have not detected activity in recent time. But old fault scars indicate that earthquakes occurred before. Geologists recognize that these faults are still active and predicted that the earth's crust could break here again. And it did! — in the identical location of the last "prehistoric quake."

Friday, October 28, 1983, the crust ruptured! The shock-registering 7.3 on the Richter scale — spread 500 miles from the focal point, or "epicenter." You are looking at the scar, or "scarp," created by the quake.

Thousand springs valley dropped about 7 1/2 feet while the lost river range rose about a foot — both in a tilted manner.

The results. The scarp before you extends for 21 miles, paralleling the mountain front. In some places, multiple scarps formed. Ground motion, or 'ground roll,' did $15 million damage to roads and buildings in the Challis and Mackay Areas. Boulders tumbled down mountains. Some struck homes around Challis 35 miles north. New springs — and craters called 'sand boils' — erupted in the valley. The largest deluge of water ever recorded after an earthquake in the United States — some 400 billion gallons — gushed forth.

We know that identical earthquakes rocked this area in the past — as recently as a few thousand years ago.

167

It will happen again! Scientists cannot say exactly when, but Borah Peak and Thousand Springs Valley will certainly slide farther apart as more earthquakes rumble along this fault system.

For more information, stop at National Forest Offices in Mackay or Challis. Challis National Forest.

When I compare this information with that given earlier at the Painted Desert Welcome Center about the continents separating, I could not resolve the differences. Is the U.S. getting bigger AND moving away from our neighbors across the Atlantic? Is the whole earth growing, or is the surface shrinking somewhere else?

Returning on Double Springs Road to US-93, I found Birch Springs Road, which took me to the parking area from which the trail leads to the summit. At the summit is a USGS survey benchmark monument and a register book, which was placed by The Mazamas of Portland, Oregon.

It is more than just a very strenuous hike since it requires scrambling (rock climbing using the hands) and crossing a small, but sometimes precipitous, snowfield at very high altitude. At least a half dozen people have died while attempting to reach the summit, so know what you're doing before leaving your bike at the parking area.

A ridge on the way to the peak is called Chicken-out Ridge. The ranger station is a good source for information. You would be wise to have special training and equipment if you intend to climb to the peak.

Borah Peak was named in honor of the late Senator William E. Borah who served in the U. S. Senate from 1907 to 1940. He was known as the Lion of Idaho. The Lost River Range, which includes Borah Peak, is a long, narrow fault block of sedimentary rock pushed up between two down-dropped blocks forming valleys. Most of the rocks that outcrop in the range are lithified ocean sediments. Fossils of bivalve shells and corals can be found high on the mountain. A worldwide flood seems the most logical explanation of why the fossils are up high but not down lower. An earthquake on October 28, 1983, left a fault scrap 21 miles long and up to 14 feet high near the western base of Borah Peak.

Highpointer Paul Lindsay has led several up to the summit. He says most people take four to six hours up and another three hours down, but the hike is pretty much straightforward from the parking lot. The trail leaves from the uphill side of the parking lot and though there is no marker, the route is evident. The forest service has installed an outhouse, and there are several campsites with tables around the parking area where the trail begins, but there is no water.

One sign, which calls it Mt. Borah reads, "Ten or a dozen large but shallow inland seas have covered this area in the past billion years. They became a graveyard for countless generations of sea creatures, bones, shells, coral, and microscopic remains piled up through the eons into a clay-and-limestone deposit thousands of feet thick. During the past ten or 20 million years, part of this deposit has been thrust upward into the towering ridge which you see before you." It never ceases to amaze me that these people are so unsure of the timing. Can you imagine telling someone in the presence of your spouse that you have been married 10 or 20 years?

ROUTE:

From Mt. Rainier in WA: Out to US12 to Yakima. I-82 to Prosser (Exit 82). SR221 to SR14 to Plymouth. I-82 and US-395 to I-84 to ID. I-84 to Exit 57 to SR21 through Idaho City to Stanley. SR75 to US-93 to Birch Springs Road (gravel) at the sign for Borah Peak access (1/4 mile north of MM 129). At about 3.3 miles the road turns and runs down the earthquake fault of 1983 for about 100 ft then passes through a wooded patch and emerges in a parking lot (680).

SIDE TRIPS:

Craters of the Moon National Monument is about 50 miles south of Mackay via US-93, US-20 and US-26. The Idaho National Energy Laboratory (atomic energy commission) is also along US-20 and US-26.

#38

Granite Peak, Montana
(12,799 feet)

Another first time experience.

W<small>HILE IN</small> A<small>RIZONA</small> (Chapter 32) I had my first meal of buffalo and now, before leaving Idaho, I experienced a bed and breakfast for the first time. Motel rooms were taken where I stopped in Rexburg, Idaho, so when the desk person asked if I wanted her to check at the B&B, which was about the same price, I said yes. There were empty beds, so I reserved one and headed out of town.

At the Porter House, I was allowed to put the Gold Wing in their large barn/storage building/garage. I liked it already. I had skipped supper, but was yearning for some popcorn and a soda. No problem, said Craig. My room was $35 with a shared bath. Breakfast was a nutritious choice of fruits, waffles, eggs, etc. Since Craig and Virginia Porter have a handful of boys, I'm sure none of the leftovers were "left over." I was the first guest who came on a motorcycle, so I tried to leave a good impression for those who might come afterward. I suggested that if they provide a hose and some simple cleaning items for washing motorcycles, they might have many more to follow. Many of us like to have clean bikes while traveling.

Leaving Rexburg the next morning took me north and through West Yellowstone into Yellowstone National Park. What a disappointment! As a young teenager, I had been to the park with my mom & dad. What a wonderful time — especially catching fish with my dad. I had also passed through the park with Jeri after we had been married a few years.

Yellowstone is the world's first, and perhaps most famous, national park, and it was celebrating its 125th anniversary in 1997. Who signed the act creating this park for the benefit and enjoyment of the people on March 1, 1872? Ulysses S. Grant, that's who. Since then, about another 375 sites in the United States have been preserved or claimed by our government. That number is still climbing. Evidently, enough people think that only our government can save beautiful landscapes. As I passed through the park, it was evident that they can't save beautiful landscapes from forest fires. With each act that sets aside parcels of land, there is a price to pay; or more precisely, a price not to collect. Not one cent of taxes has been collected in the form of property taxes on these 200 million-plus acres of real estate.

Straddling the borders of Wyoming, Montana, and Idaho, the greater Yellowstone ecosystem consists of two national parks, six national forests, three national wildlife refuges, and other federal, state, and private lands. Yellowstone is no stranger to controversy. One of more than half a dozen issues is what was most evident to me as I passed through the park: wildfires.

The first explorers to Yellowstone found landscapes largely fashioned by fire. However, during the next century, a policy of fire suppression prevailed among federal land agencies. In the 1940s, plant ecologists began to understand that fire is the primary agent of change in the arid, high-altitude West since it recycles entire plant communities. Fires quickly return nutrients to the soil and open the forest canopies to sun-loving plants. Fires also help control disease and create habitat mosaics that support greater biological diversity.

In 1988 drought, hurricane-force winds, lightning, and a fuel load centuries in the making combined to create an unprecedented fire season. About 1/3 of the park burned. Our federal government tried to protect nature and may have messed it up worse than if we had left it alone. I had better get off the subject lest you begin thinking this is an anti-government book.

Expect to pay dearly just to drive through the park. Automobiles are $20: motorcycles are $15. If you plan to visit very many federal parks in one year, you might consider the *Golden Eagle Passport*, which is $50 but allows the vehicle into all federal parks for one year from the date of purchase.

When you enter, you'll receive enough maps and newspapers to keep you from seeing anything if you keep your nose in them. It might be worth your time to pull off and at least glance through the information you just purchased. Scan for information that interests you, but be sure to read the cautions and rules. Remember that ignorance is no excuse.

In 1997 there were warnings for motorcyclists and bicyclists that roads can be very rough, with large potholes. Amen to that! I thought Michigan's roads were bad!

Climbing Granite Peak requires special training and equipment. Although the forest roads are gravel, they are maintained and are normally suited for any type vehicle.

The first ascent of Granite Peak was on August 29, 1923, by a party led by Elers Koch, who was the assistant regional forester at the time. Granite Peak was the last of the 50 state highpoints to be climbed.

Dennis Whitehead, a physician at the Marquette General Hospital, survived two days and nights of rain, snow and high winds as he awaited rescue help from Granite Peak as reported in *He Won't Forget This Vacation* by Jenny Lancour. About 100 feet from the peak, Jack Parsell of Beaver Falls, New York, (at age 66) took a ten-foot fall and broke his leg. Two of the five hikers immediately began returning down the mountainside to get help. Terry Moyer of Salt Lake City, Utah, was the third man remaining on a six-foot ledge, which slanted downward to a 100-foot drop.

They slept in shifts to make sure they didnt roll off. Sleeping bags and other supplies had been left at their 12,000-foot base camp, so they spent the first cold night telling jokes. Whitehead and Moyer did jumping jacks to stay warm and all three huddled together. On the second day, Moyer headed back down the mountain to conserve what little food and water remained and to make sure the others had gotten to safety.

What is the point of sharing the experience of these Highpointers? Accidents happen even with experienced hikers, so know what you re getting into. Did Dennis & Terry complete their climb to the peak? Yes, the day after the rescue of injured Jack Parsell.

Granite Peak was another summit I had no intentions of climbing. From US-212, I was not even sure which was Granite, but if it is visible from that road, I saw it and was as close to it as I had intended.

ROUTE:

From Borah Peak in ID: US-93 to Arco. SR33 through Mud Lake to Rexburg. US-20 to W. Yellowstone and then through Yellowstone National Park onto US-212 to MT (379).

SIDE TRIPS:

Charles Kuralt has rated the Beartooth Scenic Highway, US-212, between Red Lodge and Yellowstone National Park via Cooke City, as one of the ten most scenic highways in the US. Breathtaking, magnificent mountain scenery is at every turn (except for the miles of burned landscape).

#39

Gannett Peak, Wyoming
(13,804 feet)

Tribute to a biker.

O N THIS STRETCH of the trip I must comment on three notable events. The first was following a peaceful night of rest in Cody, Wyoming, at the KOA. While packing Thursday morning, I began talking to Brad Tresek from Savage, Maryland, who was loading his red Honda ST1100. Our conversation began with motorcycles, which led to a very interesting story. Brad was anxious to get away from the congestion of home between Baltimore, Maryland, and Washington, D.C. Brad logged 830 miles the first day and then settled down to a more enjoyable pace of seeing more. We talked about our current trips, but his story of a trip two years earlier was worth writing down. This is how Brad told it:

> I was riding my ST1100 on my first cross-country trip in August 1995. I had just come from the town of Sturgis, South Dakota, (three days before the rally started), and was traveling through the Black Hills. I had stopped at a Wal-Mart to pick up some sweats due to the fact that I had only brought two wool blankets with me. (Important lesson learned: Even in August it's very cool at night in the Western mountains.)

As I was about to walk into the store I noticed a Kawasaki 550 LTD near the entrance. The obvious owner, a woman in leather chaps and vest, was finishing a conversation on the pay phone outside. When she was done, I said to her, 'I haven't seen one of those in a long time.'

She said 'I just turned over 100,000 miles on it.'

I looked at the speedometer and couldn't believe it! This was the original engine, never been rebuilt. From then on, I was hooked. I found out she was a grandmother and was traveling alone for the summer. She has also traveled all over this country, mostly solo and all on that 550 Kawasaki. She ended up spending 103 days on the road for her '95 trip.

She told me she had been traveling through the Wind River Canyon, south of Thermopolis, when the LTD turned over the speedometer. I remember she said, 'Brad, I was standing there at the side of the road jumping up and down and taking pictures of the bike, but there was no one there to take a picture of me with it.'

We must have talked for at least 45 minutes or more about all kinds of bike 'stuff', swapping info, telling tales —well, you know how it is when you start talking 'bikes.'

Before we left, we took pictures and then she did something that took me by surprise. She said, 'Let me see your wallet.' At first I wasn't quite sure what that meant but she just said again, 'Let me see your wallet.'

Well, I did, and she took out a roll of stick-on labels with her name and address printed on them. She peeled one off, stuck it to the inside of my wallet and said, 'There! Now you can write to me and you won't lose my address.'

I visited Moxie in 1996 on a bike trip to Connecticut and saw that she had some artwork done on her bike at Sturgis that year, commemorating the occasion. She showed me the pictures she had taken and I promised her that some day I would find that spot and mark it to honor the accomplishment. This is the year to keep my promise.

Brad showed me a small picture Moxie had taken of her bike in Wind River Canyon along US20. He had recently taken a picture of his ST1100 at about the same spot and left the brass plaque pictured above in honor of her 100,000-mile accomplishment.

Later that day, I found the spot in Wind River Canyon along the east side of the road which followed the river and took a picture of our Gold Wing at the monumental place where Brad had recently placed the plate in honor of Moxie. Since I didn't have his picture with me, I located it by memory and discovered later that I was several yards from the exact spot.

The second memorable event was just before arriving at Farson, Wyoming. I had been told by Rick & Joyce Vandersloot of Rock Springs, Wyoming, to be sure to stop and have a world famous ice cream cone at the Farson Mercantile. Right! Like this little crossroads in the middle of nowhere could be famous?

Farson is at the intersection of SR28 and US191. It is literally a four-way stop with little more than an ice cream shop in an old church or something. But before talking about the ice cream, I need to tell about the two BMW sport bikes that passed me, and what followed.

I had just crossed the South Pass, enjoying perfect weather of 75-80 degrees, about a mile and a half above sea level on SR28 and heading for Farson. I was going about a mile a minute when one BMW passed me. I hadn't seen him nor the next one in my mirrors. Very little comes up from behind me without my knowledge, but maybe you'll understand why I might have missed seeing them. I decided I would run with them a while since we were headed the same direction.

The weather was clear and we could see for miles. The road was great and I rolled on the throttle. The speedometer connected to the horses between my legs was soon reading 105 mph and I rolled off the throttle a little to keep the needle there.

Being used to riding about 60 mph, the additional 45 mph was not as unsettling as I had thought it would be. Other than needing to increase the volume on my radio because of the increased wind noise, I noticed very little difference in how the Interstate handled. I took my position as third bike and settled down to keep with the two BMWs for the next 35 miles. They were cruising about 95 mph. At the four-way stop in Farson, Bob Broberg & Lou Starelli stopped for a break. I stopped because of Rick & Joyce from Wyoming's GWRRA Chapter C said that I should.

I treated Bob & Lou to an ice cream cone as we talked. They were from the Portland, Oregon, area. Bob later wrote that he was amazed that the Wing would go that fast! He obviously had not read the December 1995 issue of *Wing World*, which reported the Honda Gold Wing had established an open record in the Motorcycle Stock Production — 1650 cc class at 105.013 mph. That must mean that our speedometer registers a little high or it should be on the track. When I later filled with fuel, I figured I averaged about 22 mpg while running at 95 mph, which would be about half of the mileage I get at 60 mph.

At the Farson Mercantile, we had to stand in line to be served. There were too many vehicles and people to get a good estimate, but I was able to learn that sixteen 4x4s with four people per vehicle were doing the Oregon/Mormon Trail. I was able to talk more with the same group when we camped together at the KOA in Lyman, Wyoming, that evening.

Gannett Peak is one of the more difficult summits to climb with considerable exposure or travel on glaciers or snowfields. Training and ropes are required as well as a multi-day backpack trip on either of three routes (33-50 miles). Sudden storms with strong winds and sub-zero wind chill are common. Expect mosquitoes, deer flies, and horseflies to be plentiful most of the summer.

Gannett Peak, first climbed in 1922, was named in honor of Henry Gannett, chief topographer on the early Hayden Survey in Wyoming and a member of the U.S. Geological Survey from 1882 to 1914—a great American geographer.

This peak is on the continental divide. The continental divide is like one long mountain with several peaks of more than 13,000 feet on either side of Gannett, the highest. Several glaciers and dozens of lakes are visible on both sides of the summit divide. At the summit, in a shelter of several large granite boulders, is the registration book, placed inside a copper tube which resembles a stovepipe with a cap. Gannett Peak is surrounded by some of the most remote and scenic mountain area in the 48 contiguous states. Bridger Wilderness, on the west side, is 90 miles long and contains 383,300 acres of the 1,700,029-acre Bridger National Forest. Trout abound in many of the 1,300 lakes in Bridger Wilderness: 31 have rainbow, 71 eastern brook, 85 cutthroat, and 29 golden.

Following the completion of his 48th peak, Highpointer Rick Peterson had a report in the fourth quarter 1996 *A to Z Newsletter* about Gannett. He rates Gannett Peak "as having the most spectacular approach and being the most beautiful of the contiguous (highpoints). Thoroughly enjoyed the company of my fellow climbers. Great trip, even with a quick descent due to lightning and buzzing rocks and the loss of two climbers to a crevasse. Yes, we recovered the climbers and all made it down safely."

Though not normal, a grizzly was allegedly captured in the Pinedale area. This is no cause for alarm — just a call to realize that others are sharing their wilderness with us.

RECOMMENDED ROUTE:

From Granite Peak in MT: US-212 to Wyoming and SR296 to SR120 through Cody and Thermopolis. US-20 to Shoshoni. US-26 to Riverton to Lander. US-287 to SR28 to Farson. US-191 through Pinedale to SR352 to Bridger Wilderness. The paved road becomes gravel (386). How far you can go will depend much on weather and ever-changing road condition.

#40

Kings Peak, Utah
(13,528 feet)

One of many.

Kings Peak is a part of The High Uintas Wilderness, which was created by congress on September 28, 1984. The Forest Service was designated by Congress to protect the wilderness by ensuring there are no new buildings, roads, grazing, drilling, or timber removal. The existing changes at the time were grandfathered, so you may see some of man's improvements to the wilderness. As a visitor, you are asked to leave no evidence of your visit, which is often called the "Minimum Impact Technique."

Many peaks in this area are above 10,000 feet and seldom see 80 degrees. Nights are often 30-40 degrees during the warmer months, so from I-80 many snowfields on the slopes can be seen. This is not a hike one should attempt without much preparation. The wilderness area is quite large, so maps and the skills to read them are necessary for a climb to the summit. Those enjoying hiking company will like the Henrys Fork Trail starting at the Henry's Fork Trailhead and ending at Gunsight Pass. This is the heaviest used route leading to Kings Peak and has been conveniently broken into six sections.

Section 1 is from the trailhead to Alligator Lake turnoff. This section climbs slowly out of the river bottom, follows the river, and overlooks its clear running waters. The hiker will walk through aspen, lodgepole pine, and view numerous wildflowers as he crosses a terrace with a moderate incline. Moose and deer are often visible along the perimeter areas of forest and marsh. This section is approximately 1.5 miles and should take 40-60 minutes with a full pack.

Section 2 is marked by a series of small waterfalls on the east side of the trail then parallels the river through two long meadows. These meadows have an abundance of grasses and willows. The 2.5 miles will take at least an hour to hike.

Section 3 begins by a weather station in a wet area on the west side of the trail. From there, the path begins a steady incline and approach to the second terrace which leads to Elkhorn Crossing. Halfway up this terrace one may hear the falls, which are approximately 50 yards east of the trail. This one-mile section will take about 40 minutes to hike.

Section 4 is Elkhorn Crossing, a junction area.

Section 5 is from Elkhorn Crossing to Dollar Lake. Begin by crossing the river at the footbridge or horse crossing. Follow the trail on the east side of the river to the third terrace, again with a moderate rise in elevation. Once on top of this terrace, the trail opens into a long meadow. Gunsight Pass, Kings Peak, and the entire upper basin will be visible. The trail crosses several wet areas and two streams. The second stream comes from Dollar Lake, which sets about 300 yards off the trail to the east. Dollar Lake is heavily used. Expect to take one hour to hike this two-mile section.

Section 6 begins at Dollar Lake and extends to Gunsight Pass or branches to the west to Henry's Fork Lake, which is also heavily used. Day hiking from Dollar Lake to Gunsight Pass and then on to Kings Peak is about 4.5 miles and will require about four hours one way for this is a steep climb.

Most people take off at Gunsight Pass and go slightly uphill then follow the contour around to Anderson Pass. One hiking guidebook advises against attempting this, but it is definitely a frequently used route leading around the hill from Gunsight Pass. The key is to look carefully from Gunsight Pass and pick out the natural route above and through the first band of cliffs. Beyond the first cliffs, the terrain is less steep.

From Anderson Pass, the peak is not difficult to climb and does not require any special equipment. It does require a set of strong lungs and legs, along with a little route finding. Hikers will do a lot of boulder hopping and ledge walking. There are sharp dropoffs to the west. The route follows the ridge crest, generally on the east, and is marked by occasional cairns.

The lakes in the upper reaches of the drainage and closest to Kings Peak are heavily used both by those whose primary purpose is to climb Kings Peak and by those whose primary purpose is to catch fish. As such, anyone looking for more of a wilderness experience and some degree of solitude should consider some of the other possible routes.

A couple of different trails access the peak from the south. One begins at the Seift Creek Trailhead and the other starts at the Uinta River Trailhead. Both of these are accessible by way of Roosevelt, Utah. From these two trailheads, trails following the Uinta River and Yellowstone Creek lead visitors up to Kings Peak. These trails are not as heavily used as the Henrys Fork Trail because they are a little longer; however, the scenery is just as beautiful and are the choice of those hikers who want to avoid crowds.

ROUTE:

From Gannett Peak in WY: SR352 back to US-191 (N) to Daniel. US-189 and I-80 to Evanston. SR150 (S). Between Evanston and Kamas (250), Utah's Kings Peak should be visible to the east but it will be difficult to pick out without help since there are many peaks.

#41

Panorama Point, Nebraska
(5,424 feet)

Tri-State corner marker is nearby.

CLAUD ALDEN AND Art Henrickson discovered Panorama Point in 1951. The Kimball Chamber of Commerce installed the marker in 1971. The chamber office in Kimball will supply you a map with clear directions to Panorama Point and the nearby three-State corner marker, along with a certificate issued by the Kimball-Banner County Chamber of Commerce to commemorate your visit to Nebraska's highpoint. New signs and two cattle guards were installed in 1989 because there was concern that wire gates might be left open.

When I was on the last mile along the fence, I stopped to get a closer look at some of the bison from the H. P. Bison Ranch. Thirty-eight bison grazed along the fence. Several appeared to stand six feet tall. I had my red jacket on and had received a warning when I entered Yellowstone National Park about buffalo. Some of these animals weigh 2,000 pounds and can run at 30 miles per hour, about twice as fast as I can run when chased, so I chose not to get very close, but it was still an exciting experience.

Leaving Panorama Point, I decided to visit the nearby tri-state marker for Nebraska, Colorado and Wyoming. I turned right (south) onto Rd 5, which became Rd 111, and I entered Colorado. At about 3.4 miles from the highpoint, I turned right on Rd 136 for three miles. I turned right again on Rd 105, which was dirt until the Colorado/Wyoming states line where it was paved. There was a cattle guard on the east side of County Road 105 along a pasture trail and windmill. It is easy to see the marker about 3/4 mile off the road.

Oliver N. Chafee erected the original tri-state corner marker on August 17, 1869. Art Henrickson of Kimball built a new base around it in 1981. Even though the original marker is several hundred feet from where congress had intended it to be, the location is the official corner for the states.

What a surprise to see several vehicles and about a dozen men at the marker. The Surveyors of the 6th P. M., the Professional Land Surveyors of Wyoming, the Professional Surveyors Association of Nebraska, and the Professional Land Surveyors of Colorado, were preparing the site for a public program to dedicate the restored corner one week from the day I was there.

The "DEDICATION OF THE RESTORED CORNER MONU-MENT COMMON TO NEBRASKA AND WYOMING ON THE COLORADO LINE" was co-sponsored by the U. S. Bureau of Land Management, the survey societies of Nebraska, Colorado and Wyoming, the historical societies and citizens of Nebraska, Colorado and Wyoming, and held on site August 16, 1997. I'm often late for things, but this time I was one week early.

ROUTE:

From Kings Peak in UT: Backtrack on SR150 or continue through Kamas to pick up I-80 to NE. Exit I-80 at Bushnell Interchange 12 miles west of Kimball. Rd 17 for 10 miles, Right on Rd 8 for 4.2 miles, Left for 1 mile on Rd 9, /Right on Rd 6 for 2 miles, Left on Rd 5 for 2 miles to Henry Constable's home (before H. P. Bison ranch which is on the left). Turn right and go about a mile initially following the fence to the south/left (392).

#42

Harney Peak, South Dakota
(7,242 feet)

Slippery when wet.

B Y SATURDAY AFTERNOON I was well ahead of schedule and called another couple with whom I had only corresponded prior to this trip. Al Vogele was in Sturgis, but Lois invited me to stay with them for the weekend. Lois was going to rejoin Al Saturday evening (the end of bike week) in Sturgis where he had been busy with the Lehman Trike Conversions Display. I was unable to make it to Rapid City before she needed to leave, so we agreed to meet at the Display in Sturgis.

Al and Lois had a red Gold Wing, which Al had converted to a Lehman Trike. He is one of the authorized Lehman Trike Dealers and was joined by John and Linda Lehman and John's brother-in-law Rennie Jensen. They brought with them one BMW, one Harley and another model Honda trike so Sturgis visitors would have five Lehman trikes to examine. Mr. Lehman has been making trike conversions since about 1987.

Al & Lois gave the typical warm biker's welcome and invited me to downtown Sturgis for supper followed by a short ride among the bikes lining the streets. Plans were made for meeting the Lehmans and Rennie in the morning for a bike ride on Sunday. The meeting place was to be a gas station in Rapid City soon after breakfast.

I followed the Vogeles from Sturgis to Rapid City, where they opened their log home to me. Sundays were usually my day of rest so I could catch up on writing and doing laundry. Lois allowed me to wash and dry some clothes, but no letter writing got done. After a leisurely breakfast, Al, Lois and I headed for the meeting place. With tanks full and rain gear on, six of us, on three trikes and my two-wheeler, started our 159-mile ride through rain and fog—a chilly day, but with some great folks!

It wasn't until Monday morning that I drove up near Harney Peak. Since it had been raining and was still overcast and wet, the trail would have been a bit more difficult than hands-in-pockets hiking, so I opted to not attempt the six-mile climb. The fog still lingered from the day before so there would have been little to see.

The peak was named after General William S. Harney, the commanding officer of Lt. G. K. Warren, who mapped the peak during a military expedition to the Hills in 1857. Harney Peak is approximately eight miles north-northeast of Custer in the Black Elk Wilderness Area of Black Hills National Forest, but wilderness permits are not required. Each of the three most used trails is about six miles and considered Class 1 hiking most of the way.

The Custer Black Hills Expedition of 1874 attempted to climb Harney Peak but, according to Don W. Holmes in *Highpoints Of The United States*, darkness fell and the expedition failed. The first white man known to reach the summit was Dr. Valentine T. McGillycuddy while on the Jenny Scientific Expedition in 1875 at the age of 26. At his request, his ashes were placed in a crypt on Harney Peak in 1940 with a plaque embedded in the base of the tower steps. He played an instrumental part in the photographic and geologic mapping of the Black Hills. He later served as an agent on the Pine Ridge Reservation and as the first president of the South Dakota

School of Mines. Also engraved on the plaque are the words "*Wasicu Wakan*," meaning "holy white man.' This was an honor bestowed on McGillycuddy by the Sioux tribes, and dedicated at his interment by Thomas Lone Eagle.

There are no sanitary facilities, trashcans, or drinking water at the peak, so take water, and plan to pack out what you pack in. The shortest route to the peak is via Trail 9 from Sylvan Lake or Willow Creek Horse Camp. The round trip from Sylvan Lake takes four to five hours. Trails 2, 3, 4 and 7 also lead to 9 and the peak. The summit is a few yards west of the trail location on Harney Peak. The Civilian Conservation Corps constructed the lookout tower on the summit in 1938-39. The actual highpoint is a natural rock at the base of the tower on the southeast side, below the tower balcony. There is a pillar approximately 100 feet northwest of the tower, which may look higher than the rock at the base, however, the rock at the tower is slightly more than two feet higher than the pillar. There is no USGS benchmark on the summit.

The Sioux Indians called these mountains *Paha Sapa* meaning "Black Hills," but they are really mountains, appearing to be black from a distance because of the Ponderosa Pines. The Black Hills of South Dakota is one of the most popular summer vacation areas in the country with many scenic drives and hikes.

ROUTE:

From Panorama Pt in NE: Backtrack to I-80 then to Kimball. Take SR71 through Scottsbluff to Crawford (159). US-20 just past Chadron Municipal Airport. Take US-385 to cross the state line (196). Continue on US-385 in SD through Hot Springs to Wind Cave. Take SR87 joining Needles Hwy. to the Sylvan Lake Area (279). That will be as close as you can drive to Harney Peak.

SIDE TRIPS:

There are literally too many side trips to mention them all. On several occasions I have picked up and used the free magazines, which provide coupons, maps, area highlights, calendar of events, etc. The *Traveler Magazine* I picked up for this area contained 145 pages, probably the largest I have found.

Mt. Rushmore, the world's largest mountain carving, is approximately five miles east of Harney Peak and boasts of over two million visitors annually. Can you name the four presidents? Did you know why each was selected? A brochure from the Keystone Chamber of Commerce reports that one represents the struggle for independence (George Washington). One is a reminder of government by the people (Thomas Jefferson). The third was chosen for his ideals on equality and the permanent union of the states (Abraham Lincoln). The fourth was chosen to symbolize the 20th century role of the United States in world affairs (Theodore Roosevelt). The carving actually began on August 10, 1927, and spanned fourteen years. The total cost was just less than $1 million. When Cutzon Borglum died in 1941, his son continued the work for a short time. No carving on the mountain has been done since that time and none is planned for the future. However, a $28 million facelift is planned for the surrounding grounds. The National Park Service sponsors a special free program Memorial Day through Labor Day. It consists of a ten-minute talk given by a ranger followed by a 20-minute film. The highlight of the evening is when the sculpture is slowly exposed to light until it is fully illuminated. Early morning is the best if you want a clear picture without shadows since Mt. Rushmore faces southeast and catches the morning sun.

#43

White Butte, North Dakota
(3,506 feet)

Snakes don't like you either.

WHITE BUTTE REQUIRES a hands-in-pocket hike of about two miles. It is on the private property of Mrs. Angeline Buzalsky, who would prefer that permission be obtained to cross her property: (701) 879-6370. It was established as North Dakota's highest summit in 1961 and old Indian burial grounds have been found on White Butte. Please don't disturb them.

Ronna Bailey of Colorado climbed in September 1995 and reported in the third quarter 1996 *A to Z Newsletter* that she found the trail to be easy. Low-growth juniper bushes covered most of the Butte, but it was infested with rattlesnakes. She saw two and heard four others and said it was one of the most frightening days of her life. Did it need to be? Here's a little information about rattlesnakes taken from the same newsletter as part of an excerpt from Men's Journal of March 1995.

In an article called "Vipers, Spiders and Scorpions: A Traveler's Guide To Our Poisonous Pals," Bob Lee had provided information that venom of rattlesnakes is responsible for more deaths, more hospitalizations, and more crippling injuries than the venom of any other animal in North America. But just how significant is the danger? Rattlesnakes are among the group called pit vipers, which all have a heat sensing pit beneath each eye. This helps them track prey in darkness. Bites from even the most potent rattlesnakes rarely result in death. Since an ounce of prevention is worth a pound of cure, simply avoid snakebites. It's not that difficult since snakes generally shun people. Therefore walk heavy to give them a warning that you are there, and watch where you put your feet. Still, if it's just not your day and you are bitten, get to a hospital. Don't apply a tourniquet or ice. Don't use a snakebite kit. Don't cut the puncture wound and try to suck out the venom. In fact, there is no good first aid, but if you must do something, elevate and immobilize the limb, rest quietly, and don't freak out. Most of the popular literature on snakebites has some bad ideas. Some might suggest, for example, that you chop the head off and take it with you, but might not warn that a rattlesnake could bite up to an hour after decapitation. Insist that the doctors call the Regional Poison Control Center, which is listed in the phone book.

When I made my last left turn onto the road that would take me to the Buzalsky's farm, I stopped at the first house, which had no mailbox. Since I had no answer when I knocked on the doors I almost gave up, but am glad I tried next door, which is the correct place.

On my afternoon outing I received a welcome from two folks who pointed the way and said to enjoy the hike. By the time I parked the bike, they were about their business. One headed out the driveway and the other was back inside. I feel bad that I didn't get their names. As I left the Wing heading toward the summit, I tried to stay on paths or along a fence where crops were planted in the fields.

Unlike Ronna Bailey, I neither saw nor heard any rattlesnakes. From the summit I took a picture looking eastward toward the Buzalsky farm and the house to its south where I first stopped. By the time I started my return trip from the summit, I wasn't thinking so much about rattlesnakes and could enjoy the walk a little more.

ROUTE:

From Harney Peak in SD: US-385 to Pluma. US-85&US-14A to Cheyenne Crossing. Stay on US-14A through Savoy to Spearfish. Leave Spearfish on US-85 to ND. (Stop at the Geographical Center of US about 30 miles north of Spearfish). Continue on US-85 to Township Road crossing. (Between mile markers 108 and 109. On the west side of the road is a sign for Brown's Angus Ranch). Turn right and go 4 miles then left 3.7 miles to the Buzalsky farm (230) on the left (second house).

#44

High Point, Iowa
(1,670 feet)

Now it is named Hawkeye Point.

I HAD TRAVELED ALMOST 250 miles before my hike up to White Butte and was looking forward to more than twice that many more to High Point, Iowa. I decided to carry on and stay ahead of schedule.

That idea reminded me of a poem I recalled about 'carrying on the good fight' and I started thinking that would also apply to long, difficult rides. This was among the longest legs of my trip and seemed like the slowest to pass. Was I anxious for the trip to end? I don't think that was it. Maybe it was the anticipated gathering at my final highpoint with several family members and a friend. The words for the following poem came in the months that followed.

Perseverance
by Jim Mick

It's easy to ride when everything's right,
When the temperature's great and so's the road;
It's easy to cheer when a goal is near,
Or to chat with folks about your load.

It's a different song when things go wrong,
When you're feeling infernally whipped;
When it's a hundred and three on the bank's sign,
Buck up, fellow biker, don't quit!

Be safe, but carry on!
You may be losing strength in your legs,
Or glaring of sun is starting to blind.
You're sweaty, yet dry, but never you mind.
Be safe, and carry on!
You knew some stretch would be a difficult leg,
You may look like death, but while you've a breath
Carry on, my friend! Press on!

When trav'ling along on the trip of your life,
It's easy to ride when you're comfee.
It's easy to slow, then look, lean and roll
When the dawn of your trip is beginning.
But to be one who rides in rain or heat
With a smile, there's one who inspires;
The one who can ride to Heaven's own height
Is the one who rides though he's tired.

Iowa's highpoint is on the private property of Merrill and Donna Sterler. I arrived at the Sterler farm almost three hours ahead of my schedule. Finding no one home was a disappointment because I had read that Highpointer Rick Peterson had a very enjoyable hour and a half visit with the Sterlers when he was there. On a subsequent trip with five other motorcyclists, I was able to meet Donna, who grew up on the farm, moved away, and then returned with her husband in 1954.

In 1971 an U. S. Geological Survey topological engineer's crew found Iowa's highpoint behind the Sterler's barn. Prior to that survey, Ocheyedan Mound, about four miles south and nine miles east of Iowa's true highpoint, was considered highest but in fact is 57 feet lower. Ocheyedan Mound is more prominent and was used by Indians as an observation point and place of mourning. Early settlers also used Ocheyedan Mound as a guide across the prairie.

There is no USGS benchmark at the highpoint, but Mr. Sterler has placed his expired Iowa license plate "HIGH PT" on the cattle-feeding trough. The Sterlers would prefer that permission be obtained to cross their property (phone number is (712) 754-2045). However, in the event no one is home to grant permission, it is not mandatory. They welcome visitors and provide free key chains (one per family) to those who visit. Remember that the Iowa highpoint is on private property, so please respect the rights of the owners. The large water tower labeled *Osceola Rural Water* is approximately 150 yards north of the highpoint.

Although I wasn't in Iowa long, I picked up a brochure produced by the Iowa Farm Bureau Federation Ag Leadership and Promotion Foundation which boasted that Iowa was number one in pork production and raises 25 percent of the hogs in the U.S. There are literally more hogs in Iowa than people in New York City! Breakfast at a local restaurant should include sausage, ham or bacon unless you want to have the ultimate — a pork chop. A 220-pound market hog provides 122 pounds of meat. Not to be known only for hogs, Iowa is also the number one corn-producing state in the nation. About 20 percent of the corn grown in the U.S. comes from Iowa. Then there are also crops of soybeans. Depending on the year, Iowa ranks number one or two in soybean production.

Cattle are another popular sight on the farms or Iowa. Almost 1.5 million head of beef cattle are raised each year for the meat they produce. Other dairy cattle are used for milk production. The average Iowa dairy cow produced six gallons of milk a day, but some of the very best cows can produce as much as 17 gallons a day. When processed, five gallons of milk equal 1.4 pounds of butter or four pounds of cheese.

Corn deserves to be mentioned since more than 3/4 of all food items in the grocery store contain corn products. You may even add corn to your gas tank. When you fill with gas, you may notice an ethanol label on the pump, which means the gas is blended with a corn product (usually 10 percent).

ROUTE:

From White Butte in ND: Back to US-85 to Bowman. US-12 to Ortley, SD. I-29 to Sious Falls, SD. I-90 to Luverne, MN. US-75 to Rock Rapids, IA. SR9 to Sibley. SR60 2 miles to a road on the right leading toward the water tower. The Sterler farm is on the right (558).

#45

Charles Mound, Illinois
(1,235 feet)

*Ownership changed
hands recently, and may again.*

ALTHOUGH CHARLES MOUND is southeast of what is now called Hawkeye Point in Iowa, almost all of the roads I used went east or south, so if you trace my route you'll see it appears to be steps across Iowa. The exception was a stretch of about 11 miles heading southeast from Dubuque, Iowa, to Galena, Illinois on US20. Details on my map do not identify the road shown between Galena to Charles Mound, and the two books I used for this trip only helped a little. One called it Stagecoach Road while the other called it Stagecoach Trail. Both books identified it as a County Road, but only one gave the number CR67. My Map-N-Go software program identified the road from Galena to Charles Mound as CR3, so I stopped two places in Galena for help.

When I arrived at the Visitor Information Center and Chamber of Commerce, located in an old building next to the railroad tracks, it was just before closing and almost all of the dozen-or-so parking spots were full. And that was the middle of the week! Galena is a historical river town dating back to the

early 1800s with more than just the two points of interest indicated on my map (Ulysses S. Grant's home, and Old Market
House). Many of the buildings were constructed from 1826 to
1845, an era when 83 percent of the nation's lead was produced in the Galena area.

According to *Fifty State Summits* by Paul L. Zumwalt,
Elijah Charles built a log house for his family at the base of the
mound in 1828 and since that time this highpoint has been
known as Charles Mound.

> During the early years, marauding bands of Sac and
> Fox Indians led by Chief Blackhawk caused so much
> anxiety and fear that settlers built a blockhouse on
> Charles Mound for protection. Attacks were so fre-
> quent and surprising that five families took refuge in
> the fort for one entire summer, and no crops could be
> planted that season.

> There is a replica of the old fort and a small building
> housing museum items and mementos from the high-
> est points in several states. Displaced tombstones
> from the community area with burial dates from 1833
> to 1860 have been collected and are being preserved
> in respectful memory and tribute to all pioneer fami-
> lies.

According to Don W. Holmes in his book *Highpoints of the
United States*, White Oak Fort was once located on Charles
Mound to protect the Kellogg Trail, an old stagecoach and
wagon road so that must be the old fort's name.

In March 1987, Charles Mound was part of a 216-acre farm
owned by the John Glanville estate. It was a private park
opened to the public.

In 1993 the property surrounding Charles Mound was for
sale, and one of the owner families was living on the property.
The gentleman's name was John Hickman and asked to be
contacted to obtain permission to enter the property. Mr.
Hickman requested visitors not to block the gate at the main

road and also suggested that they be aware of the bull in the pasture. He had been charging $3 per vehicle to visit the high-point.

As of December 1994, the new owners of Charles Mound were Wayne and Jean Wuebbels. They live at Scales Mound, Illinois, (815) 845-2625, and ask that visitors sign their register. They no longer charge visitors.

When I arrived, a sign in front of the house read: "Hi-Pointers Please park here on gravel roadway and continue by foot." The summit is about 100 yards beyond the sign for park-ing and up a slight incline. The view to the south while making the 100-yard hike was as beautiful as the view to the north from the summit.

In addition to a pair of lawn chairs at the summit, I found the Charles Mound guest register with a written welcome from Wayne and Jean. About 50 yards southeast of the summit is a U.S. Geological Survey benchmark. A tree and sign also iden-tify the highpoint. When I visited Charles Mound, in addition to the signs identifying the highpoint, a number of other signs addressed the fact that Charles Mound was again for sale, but no one was home.

ROUTE:

From Hawkeye Point in IA: SR60 to SR9 to Estherville. SR4 to Pocahontas. SR3 to Hampton. US-65 to US-20 through Dubuque to Galena. Stagecoach Trail about 11 miles to Elizabeth-Scales Mound Rd (CR4) about 1 mile to Charles Mound Rd/Ave. The gate will be to the left and the driveway to the house is about a mile long (362).

#46

Timms Hill, Wisconsin
(1,951 feet)

Big goof!

Aᴼᴛᴇʀ ʟᴇᴀᴠɪɴɢ Cʜᴀʀʟᴇꜱ Mound about suppertime, I quickly found myself in Wisconsin, and the countryside continued to change from cornfields to hilly dairy farms. The weather was perfect, but the radio stations made me aware that things would be different the next day when I would arrive at Timms Hill.

During your travels, especially in the country, have you ever wondered what is happening when you see a small black bird or two playing 'dodge-em' with a hawk or some other larger bird? I have often speculated and figured it was likely NOT their young learning to fly or just playing with mom or dad. Could it be the larger bird has food, which the smaller birds are attempting to steal? I've seen that with sea gulls and a few other same-size birds. I had the opportunity to ask Gary Richmond that very question. Gary is a wonderfully enjoyable *Father Nature* who has served as a camp naturalist, worked at the Los Angeles Zoo, and has written more than two dozen books about what God has created in nature.

Gary said the smaller birds are often mocking birds. These

are very territorial and don't like the intrusion by the larger bird, so by annoying the larger bird they hope to drive it away. If it is a hawk they are bothering, they may very well be trying to protect their nest by distracting the hawk whose eyesight is so keen. Then I remembered that many years ago the red-winged blackbirds would dive-bomb me on portions of my paper route when I was too near to their nest. It made sense to me.

I know that it has happened to virtually every adult, but I probably feel my lowest when I forget plans to meet with someone, never more than when they go out of their way to meet with me. Before my departure from Michigan, more than a month earlier, my sister Barb said that she, my brother-in-law Roger, and maybe a couple others would plan to meet me for a picnic at Timms Hill. How did I forget? I don't know how.

Plans had been made for several, including Barb and Roger, to meet me at my final highpoint just two days later. Did that cause me to forget to meet them at Timms Hill? The weather was cool (55 degrees) and wet, but I was seven hours ahead of schedule when I arrived. If I had remembered I would have called Barb & Roger at their home in Shawano, Wisconsin, and either arranged to meet earlier or I would have slowed my pace, but I didn't remember.

Timms Hill is approximately six miles east of Ogema within the county park bearing its name. I found ample signs directing me to the summit and arrived at 11 am wearing my winter down jacket under my red GWRRA Chapter A jacket, which helped keep the chill from reaching my bones. Just about the time I was convinced Timms Hill had no apostrophe, I would find a few more official things, including the area signs, indicating Timm's Hill instead of Timms Hill. One of the signs near the summit says:

> This is the Northern Terminus of the Timm's Hill National Trail. The Secretary of the Interior, Manuel Lujan Jr., designated the ten-mile path on March 21, 1990, as the first side trail pursuant to the National

Trail System Act. Volunteers from the High Point Ski Club constructed the trail southward from this point in 1986.

The trail is open for non-motorized public use to its junction with the ice age national scenic trail in Taylor County.

There was a sawmill in operation on Timms Hill from 1898 until 1907. Timms Hill was last logged in 1944. Price County (whose Tourism Department includes the apostrophe) purchased the land in 1978 and the County Park was completed in November 1982. The summit tower was also completed at that time and overlooks the park of almost 200 acres. Timms Lake and Bass Lake are near the summit and can both be seen from the tower.

A *National Geographic* article of March 26, 1909 identified Rib Hill at 1940 feet as the highest elevation in Wisconsin. As with many states, when methods improved in determining elevations, the error was discovered and Timms Hill now holds that designation of Wisconsin's highpoint. If you are going to stay overnight in the area, High Point Village is a place to consider. It is *the place* if you're looking for a quiet little hide away.

I was long gone from Timms Hill by the time Barb and Roger left Shawano. Barb has been teaching piano in Shawano since Roger retired from the Air Force in 1977. My sister was instrumental in bringing a "judging-testing" program for piano students to Shawano in 1998. The program in not really a competition because students are not compared to each other. Instead, students earn points and awards individually, which encourages them to do well individually. With as many at 80 students each week, she had to make special arrangements with her students to meet me. Roger also had to make special plans because he drives a school bus - even during the summer when most kids are out of school. Since I was not there when they arrived and didn't show up by the time they headed home, they didn't know if I was behind schedule, lost, or what. Much later, Barb confirmed that it never crossed their minds that I just forgot. They thought I had traffic or mechanical problems. Barb and Roger ended up taking home my portion of the delicious home-cooked meal they brought to share.

ROUTE:

From Charles Mound in IL: Hwy O to Shullsburg. SR11 to SR23 through Mineral Point to Reedsburg. SR33 to Elroy. SR80 through Necedah to Pittsville. SR13 through Marshfield to Ogema. SR86 east about 5 miles to Road C to Rustic Road #62 and the Timms Hill Park entrance (291).

#47

Eagle Mountain, Minnesota
(2,301 feet)

So many choices!

O<small>NCE THE BIKE IS</small> dirty, damp weather on a motorcycle isn't so bad if the weather is warm, but when I left Timms Hill just after noon, it was only 55 degrees. Expecting to meet many of my family at my final highpoint, I pressed on. Unless you have ridden long distances in damp weather at 55 degrees, you may be unaware of how penetrating the cold can be. I was wearing the wool knit sweater my mother made in addition to my winter down coat to kept warm. It wasn't raining hard enough to require my rain gear, so I kept warm, but my coat stayed damp. That all changed as I got close to the shore of Lake Superior. The sky opened up and I was drenched by the time I stopped for the night in a motel. I decided to take a room for two nights since I would be returning this way after visiting Eagle Mountain. I spread my wet clothes over lamps, chairs, and heater vents before I took advantage of a hot bath.

The weather had improved by morning, but I still had sprinkles from time to time and it was still rather chilly.

IMPRESSIVE — my word for the harbor at Superior, Wisconsin, and Duluth, Minnesota. I could enjoy spending a day or two there! If a harbor doesn't light your fire, maybe the 30-mile ride above Duluth on Skyline Drive would do it for you. This seems to be a typical problem for motorcyclists: How do we choose where to take side trips and how long will they take?

From Duluth I chose the more scenic SR61 along the shore of Lake Superior. About 20 miles up the shore, the scenic and expressway route 61 meet at Two Harbors, Minnesota. The blacktop was great and numerous pull-off areas allowed looks at and pictures of the super Superior shoreline. With plenty of camping opportunities along the shore, how would one choose from so many? Early Friday morning signs of "No Vacancy" and "Full" tell that reservations would be a good idea.

When I arrived at the parking lot near Eagle Mountain, I was wearing my wool sweater, down coat, and rain gear. Had I learned a lesson or was I still trying to warm my bones from the day before? Maybe I had learned a lesson. I still had warm memories of the long hot bath before going to sleep the night before.

In 1996, the Highpointers Club had their 10th Annual Konvention in this area. Having made this hike then, I knew I didn't want to take my rain gear with such a light, occasional sprinkle, so I left it on the bike along with my down coat. I did wear the wool sweater — remember from chapter one that wool helps to keep us warm even when it is wet.

It was 12:25 pm when I arrived at the summit this time. Evidently the weather kept the less serious hikers from attempting the hike.

Eagle Mountain is about 17 miles northwest of the beautiful harbor town of Grand Marais in the Boundary Waters Canoe Area Wilderness of Superior National Forest. This forest contains more than 300,000 acres of clear, cold lakes and streams scattered through over two million acres. It is an easy 6.4-mile climb by trail from the parking lot and permits are not required for day hikers. The view from Eagle Mountain is excellent but the mosquitos can drive you away, so be prepared.

If you seek other directions, you may find reference to Forest Road 153, which now appears to be signed as Forest Road 170.

A plaque at the summit reads,

When Newton H. Mitchell, Minnesota's State Geologist and Ulysses S. Grant (the president's son) surveyed this area in the 1890s, they concluded that a peak in the Misquah Hills was the state's highest point. Using an aneroid barometer, they set the elevation as 2,230 feet. Later comers argued that Eagle Mountain, which Mitchell and Grant did not measure, and which can be seen from the Misquah Hills, was higher. In 1961, a United States Department of Interior survey team remeasured, using aerial photographs and controlled benchmarks. They found Eagle Mountain's elevation to be 2,301 feet making it Minnesota's highest point. They also determined that the first Misquah Hills highest peak is surpassed by another unnamed summit 2266 feet above sea level located in section 19 of T 63 N R1 W in the same western Cook County area. The state's lowest point is on Lake Superior, which has an elevation of 602 feet...

ROUTE:

From Timms Hill in WI: SR86 to Ogema. SR 13 to Ashland. US2 to Duluth and SR61 to Grand Marais. North on CR12 (Gunflint Trail) 3.6 miles. Turn left on CR8 for 5.7 miles. Turn right on CR27 which is a gravel road.

#48

Mount Arvon, Michigan
(1,979 feet)

Mini-Family Reunion.

A TRIPLE BIRTHDAY celebration was to occur along with the hiking to my last of the 48 highpoints on this trip. My brother Ted brought his wife Jan (birthday the day before), my wife Jeri, our Mom (birthday on that day) and Dad. The third birthday was mine on the next day. After work on Friday, our youngest son Jason and his best friend Brian Boers left the Detroit area and joined "The Midnight Ride of Paul Revere." That annual motorcycle fund-raiser ride left at midnight on Friday from Grand Rapids, Michigan, headed for the Mackinac Bridge.

The mighty Mackinac Bridge spans about five miles across the Straits of Mackinac, connecting the upper and lower peninsulas of Michigan while it separates Lakes Michigan and Huron. It is one of the safest and most beautiful spans ever built. Thirty-three marine foundations support the four-mile long uninterrupted steel superstructure. It was called the bridge that couldn't be built. The bridge bows or swings out to the east or west as much as 20 feet on windy days and the towers move north and south towards and away from each other as much as 18 feet, depending on the weight of the vehicles at different points across the bridge. As part of the Michigan tradition, an annual bridge walk is held on Labor Day each year, attracting tens of thousands to participate with the Governor. History buffs will want to spend the day in the area.

But is it MACKINAC or MACKINAW? You will see it both ways, and here's why. The Natives, who were the original people of the area, called the area MICHINNIMAKINONG. They also called it the "Land of the Great Turtle" because the Mackinac Island resembled a turtle. When the French arrived from the north in 1715 they corrupted the "nn" sound with an "l" and also replaced the soft "sh" sound with the "ch". The ending was heard and pronounced as "aw" by the French, but in their spelling it became the "ac." So the French called the area Michilimackinac. You'll see that name a few places. When the British came from the south and defeated the French, they heard the term pronounced as "aw" and eventually shortened it to Mackinaw. Thus you will see on the map Mackinaw City and Mackinac Island, but Mackinaw City is the only one correctly spelled with "aw." Mackinac Island, Fort Mackinac, Mackinac County, the Straits of Mackinac and Mackinac Bridge are all correctly spelled with "ac," but whichever way you see it spelled — "ac" or "aw" — it is always pronounced MACKINAW! Don't get frustrated when you see other spellings. Some people don't care or don't pay attention and much of it doesn't make any sense to outsiders. For example, check out the spellings of the Mackinac Point Light, which was built in 1892 in Mackinaw City, and decommissioned in 1957 when the lights of the Mackinac Bridge made it unnecessary.

At the end of "The Midnight Ride of Paul Revere" Saturday morning, Jason and Brian left that police escorted group and continued to L'Anse, arriving about suppertime. They were whipped when they arrived, having had only a couple of naps since the morning of the previous day.

My sister Barb and her husband Roger caught up with me

at my final highpoint. Remember that I had forgotten they had plans to meet me at Timms Hill in Wisconsin two days earlier. I had arrived early and was long gone when they arrived at Timms Hill. Their oldest son Mike with his wife Angie and their two children Ian and Mara were planning to meet us there also — COMING ALL THE WAY FROM NEW JERSEY!

The evening was getting late but Mike and Angie had not arrived yet. Our small caravan of vehicles drove into L'Anse where we visited briefly with Steve Koski at the Indian County Sports store. He has been very helpful in assisting others in the quest for finding the nearby highpoint, but since I had been there the previous year with three others, I thought I would be able to find the mailbox and marker with little help. He had not been up recently but was not aware of any problems. I didn't pay much attention to what he did say, and already had a copy of the map he provides at the store.

As we headed out of L'Anse on Main Street, which became Skanee Road, I recognized many sights. As we passed Sawmill Road (gravel) I considered taking that short cut to Roland Lake Road. Instead, we continued to the Zion Lutheran Church where we turned onto Roland Lake Road. I was very comfortable (but too cocky) with the route well past the Gravel Pit where the old logging road gradually got more difficult to ride and drive on. Another car was now at the end of our little caravan. They didn't offer to pass when they had the chance, so I just continued on. When ruts were too deep to continue, I pulled to the side and parked the Gold Wing. Ted was unable to get off the logging road (more like a path by now). Roger was able to get partially off the path and then we discovered the other car that had joined us was Mike and his family.

Dad didn't feel up to making a hike. I wasn't sure how close we were to the summit — maybe a mile. He waited with the cars and Gold Wing while the rest of us began walking up the logging trail in search of the highpoint. That was Mom's 84th birthday and she wanted to reach Mt. Arvon with her youngest son.

We were gone from Dad and the vehicles for one and a half-hours and never did find the summit. I had been too confident and not taken to heart the typical warning: "Due to logging operations, the roads in the Mt. Arvon area are frequently changed. The roads S of Skanee Road become impassible in winter due to snow. During the rainy season, the roads become muddy and are often unfit for passenger cars." With darkness falling, we gave up the quest at 8:15 pm and returned to dad and the vehicles. Returning to L'Anse, we picked up a cake, ice cream, and all the fixings for our birthday party back at the motel.

I could tell that Mom was disappointed that we didn't make it to the summit, but not as disappointed if some of us made it and she didn't. Our Mom put a lot of effort into the hike that day. Her hip and back aren't as good as years gone by, and a 1/4 mile-hike is about enough to exhaust her. I have no idea how far we walked in that 90 minutes, but it was way beyond her comfort zone. It would have been one thing if I were alone and did not find the summit, as was the case with Virginia, but to have several others depending on my leadership — I felt very bad. On my last highpoint I think I learned a valuable lesson to take the directions in hand and follow them.

For years, Mt. Curwood in Baraga County was recognized as the highest point in Michigan. In 1982, however, the U. S. Department of Interior's Geological Survey team gathered new measurements and found Mt. Curwood to be slightly lower in elevation than nearby Mt. Arvon. Mt. Curwood measured 1978.24 feet above sea level and Mt. Arvon registered at 1979.238 feet above sea level. Mt. Curwood was named for Michigan writer/naturalist James Oliver Curwood, a popular adventure novelist. The source of Arvon's name remains shrouded in mystery.

Within six months of our visit, Representative Greg Kaza reported to the Highpointers Club that Michigan has accepted a gift of perpetual easement to the peak of Mt. Arvon. The gift of easement was granted by the Mead Paper Company, which has extensive land holdings in Michigan's upper peninsula where Mt. Arvon is located. Mr. Kaza had introduced a bill in the Michigan House of Representatives in the fall of 1996 directing the DNR to open negotiations with the owner of the peak for the purpose of acquiring the land as a state park. Mead Paper quickly contacted his office and offered to spare the state the expense of purchasing the property by offering a gift of perpetual easement. Thank you Mead Paper Company and Representative Kaza!

Most of the state highpoints have been designated as county, state or federal parks. I'm not convinced that is always a good thing. I very much enjoyed several on private property like the Sterler's Farm in Iowa, White Butte in North Dakota , and the property for sale including Charles Mound in Illinois, but when I consider the property owner in Rhode Island, I understand there would be benefit of state ownership in some places. One thing for sure, property owned by private persons or companies would be paying taxes. When land belongs to the county, state or federal government, no taxes are collected on it, in fact that probably adds to the burden and expense of the government to manage.

There were two sighting reports of a female black bear with cubs in the area during 1996. No problems — just sightings. Make noise as you hike to let her know you're in her area. We made plenty of noise. It was like a mini-family reunion with 14 of us on the logging trails — looking for Mt. Arvon, but none of the noise was Mom complaining.

ROUTE:

From Eagle Mountain in MN: SR61 to Duluth. US-2 past Ironwood to Wakefield. Take SR28 to Covington. Take US-141 to L'Anse. Visit the Indian County Sports store in L'Anse for an update on directions. From L'Anse head northeast on Main Street, which will become Skanee Road. About 16 miles out of town, turn right at the Zion Lutheran Church onto Roland

Lake Road (365). Don't count on my directions to get you there from this point — remember I couldn't find it the second time.

SIDE TRIPS:

You MUST stop at the Hilltop Restaurant on the east side of US141 just south of L'Anse to have their world-famous cinnamon roll. When I stopped on a previous visit, I couldn't finish the cinnamon roll in one sitting so I finished it the next day when I got to the Mackinac Bridge. It was still very good.

#49

Epilogue

What's next?

AFTER MT. ARVON'S adventure, Mike, Angie, Ian, and Mara followed Barb and Roger back to Shawano, Wisconsin, while the rest of us headed for Frankfort, Michigan, where Ted and Jan live. Mom and Dad were taken home to nearby Beulah, Michigan, and Jeri got back to her car. Following church Sunday morning, Jeri, Jason, Brian and I returned safely to our homes northeast of Detroit.

I hope that sharing this trip of a lifetime by writing a 60,000-word book that includes several pictures will lead to others making plans to visit highpoints. **Just as a picture is worth a thousand words, a trip is worth a thousand pictures.**

My Dad said that a blessing shared is twice a blessing. I know that to be true and want Jeri to see what she missed, so we have started making plans to visit all the highpoints in the summer of 2002. She took the Motorcycle Safety Course in 2000 and is becoming comfortable riding her own motorcycle. If things continue to go well, maybe she will be able to visit the highpoints while riding her own motorcycle. That trip might roughly trace this *High On A Wing* trip but *must* include the Highpointers Konvention scheduled for late July, in Oklahoma. I might need to retire from driving for Schneider or take a leave of absence since we would have a much slower pace. Jeri also thinks she would like to do it in three phases with a short stay at home between each. That's one way to make a 15,333-mile trip into even more miles. She's beginning to think like Dean (Chapter 32)!

What would that venture look like? Motorcycling in the South is more enjoyable when not so hot and humid so that would be the place to go in the spring. Starting with Indiana and Kentucky would put us far enough south to be into warmer spring weather. Virginia, the Carolinas, Tennessee, Georgia, Florida, Alabama, Mississippi, Arkansas, Louisiana, Texas and Missouri would complete *phase one*. That would allow for riding some of Route 66 after visiting the highpoint of Texas en route to Missouri's highpoint, which should tempt more of you than just Howard (Chapters 13 & 14) to join us.

Phase two would be the out West. Those plans would include the Konvention in Oklahoma during late July and leave just the Northeast states for August.

If you have enjoyed this book, maybe we can do another version with more trivia and from two perspectives — Jeri's and mine. It would be on motorcycles, but Jeri would be riding her own. Maybe the next book would be called *Two On Two To Highpoints*.

The chairman of the Highpointers Club considers the most serious issue facing the club is maintaining access to highpoints on private land. If you intend to visit Rhode Island, please do so only on an *Access Date* arranged between the owners near the highpoint and the Highpointers Club. *Access Dates* are posted at www.highpointers.com. The owners of Kentucky's highpoint require a signed waiver (a copy of which is at the end of this book) be mailed to them before any visit on their private property. If you attempt to access the summit without a prior waiver, you risk the possibility of being prosecuted for trespassing. When visiting, only the road to the highpoint may be traveled and, as always, respect private property.

Waiver agreement for access to the summit of Black mountain, Kentucky

The undersigned ("Visitor"), for and in consideration of the access to private property granted to the undersigned by Penn Virginia Coal Company, Inc., hereby agrees as follows:

1. Visitor agrees to stay on the roadway marked on the map attached hereto as Exhibit A (page 218) and understands and agrees that the access granted to Visitor is limited to such a roadway. Visitor understands and agrees that entry into any areas outside those marked on the map as Exhibit A will be a trespass, and Visitor will be prosecuted for any such trespass.

2. Visitor, for him or herself, his or her heirs, successors, personal representatives, and assigns, hereby waives, holds harmless, and releases the owners of each and every interest, including coal lessees and coal operators and their contractors ("Owners") in the property to be visited ("Property") from and against all and any damage or injury to Visitor's person or property, including Visitor's death, regardless of the cause of such damage or injury, including any injury or damage which may result from negligence, gross negligence, criminal negligence, or criminal act of any Owner or employee, agent or representative thereof, or of any other person or entity.

3. Visitor recognizes that there may be hidden, latent, or undisclosed dangers on the Property and assumes all risks therefrom and ENTERS THE PROPERTY AT VISITOR'S OWN RISK. Visitor further recognizes that the roadway marked on Exhibit A is not maintained for public travel and may not be passable by passenger car or four-wheel drive vehicle. Visitor assumes all risk to any damage (regardless of cause) to Visitor's vehicle or other personal property.

4. Visitor agrees to abide by all safety rules and regulations imposed by any Owner of the Property, and further agrees to obey and abide by any statutory or regulatory requirements imposed upon any Owner of any interest in the Property by any state, federal or local governmental or regulatory agency.

5. Visitor agrees to conduct any and all of Visitor's activities on the Property in such a way as to interfere with any business activities being conducted on the Property.

6. Visitor agrees that Visitor will not, under any circumstances, nor at any time, assert that the Property, or any part thereof is, has become or should be deemed a "public park" as that term defined at KRS Chapter 350 and the regulations promulgated pursuant thereto.

7. Visitor states he or she is over eighteen years of age, understands the terms and conditions of this Waiver Agreement and executes it willingly, voluntarily, knowingly, and intending to be bound thereby in all respects.

OR

Visitor is a minor under the age of eighteen (18), and this Waiver Agreement is executed by such minor Visitor's parent or guardian on behalf of such minor Visitor willingly, voluntarily, knowingly and with the intention that both the minor Visitor and the parent or guardian will be bound thereby in all respects.

Witness	"Visitor"	Date
	Name of Minor Visitor	
Witness	Parent or Guardian	Date

Please sign and return to: Penn Virginia Coal Company, Attn: Steve Looney, P.O. Box 386, Duffield, VA 24244

Exhibit "A" — Map of Route to the Summit of Black Mountain, Kentucky

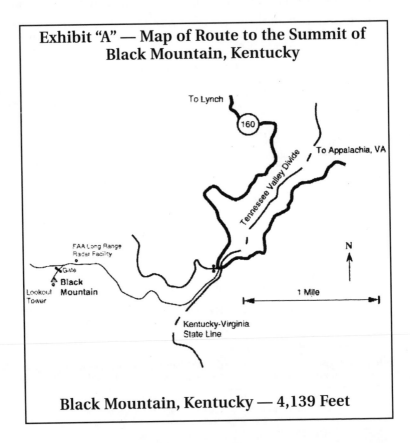

Black Mountain, Kentucky — 4,139 Feet